Praise for *Never Really Left*

"A naturally left-brained thinker, Wendy has approached her grief with a deep intellectual curiosity, studying extensively with and about some of the most respected experts in the afterlife community. Along the way, she has also given back, supporting and guiding other bereaved parents walking similar paths. Through dedicated research and personal experience, Wendy has gathered compelling evidence that our loved ones' souls continue to exist—joyful, healthy, and at peace. Meanwhile, those of us still on this side are here to learn, grow, and prepare for our own eventual reunion. In *Never Really Left*, Wendy offers tools to recognize the signs our loved ones send us, navigate the grieving process, and embrace a life of healing, gratitude, and renewed purpose. I wholeheartedly recommend her work to anyone seeking comfort, connection, and hope."

—Elizabeth Boisson, president and
cofounder, Helping Parents Heal, Inc.

"Wendy's thoughtful reflection on her journey with the afterlife, and her continued connection with her beloved son Hugh, is a profoundly moving and illuminating experience. In the face of loss, many of us secretly yearn for a sense of connection that transcends time and space. This book offers just that: a reminder that love does not end with physical separation. For anyone who has lost someone dear, this is the book you need to pick up. It beautifully explores the bond between souls, those in physical form and those in the nonphysical, reaching toward one another in a continuation and deepening of our most sacred relationships."

—Marie Manuchehri, RN, author of *Intuitive Self-Healing* and *How to Communicate with Your Spirit Guides*

"Wendy Saffel's analytical mind and insatiable desire to learn and understand whatever she focuses on proves to be the *exact* qualities necessary to synthesize the experience of grief and the journey that many explore in their healing, both scientifically and spiritually, to prove life is continuous beyond bodily death. By sharing her own journey through grief and loss, she takes her reader on a journey through the world of afterlife studies, spiritual awareness, and mediumistic unfoldment, and shares practical steps to support those who are also on this journey. It is truly the launching-off point for anyone seeking the truth of life after death, written in an easy-to-follow, relatable, and grounded perspective. I absolutely recommend this book to anyone seeking a guide through the process of the loss of a loved one and those curious to answer the question: Are my loved ones still with me, and do they go on? The evidence for life after death, when brought together the way Wendy has so masterfully done, can't be ignored. There is no one-size-fits-all evidence of survival after death that will take someone from skeptic to believer to knowing that we continue on, but Wendy's book lays out so many avenues of evidence that one (or several) of the topics she covers may lead to healing and transformation. I cannot recommend it enough!"

—Michael Mayo, medium, teacher, author, and founder of The Oakbridge Institute, Center for Mediumistic & Psychical Studies

"Packed with insights, the journey of a mother who is afforded unusual opportunities to experience her son in a different way . . . is a powerful saga. It deserves widespread attention and delivers thought-provoking moments of realization and recovery for readers, libraries, and book clubs alike."

—*Midwest Book Review*

Never
Really Left

Never Really Left

Grief, Healing, and a Mother's Unexpected Relationship with Her Departed Son

Wendy Jordan Saffel

GFB

Published by GFB™, Seattle
www.girlfridayproductions.com

Produced by Girl Friday Productions

Cover design: Emily Weigel
Production editorial: Kylee Hayes
Project management: Emilie Sandoz-Voyer

Image credits: cover © Shutterstock/Alena Gerasimova

ISBN (paperback): 978-1-967510-14-6
ISBN (ebook): 978-1-967510-15-3

Library of Congress Control Number: 2025914334

First edition

Contents

Death Is Nothing at All

BY HENRY SCOTT-HOLLAND

Death is nothing at all.
It does not count.
I have only slipped away into the next
    room.
Nothing has happened.

Everything remains exactly as it was.
I am I, and you are you,
and the old life that we lived so fondly to-
    gether is untouched, unchanged.
Whatever we were to each other, that we
    are still.

Call me by the old familiar name.
Speak of me in the easy way which you
    always used.
Put no difference into your tone.
Wear no forced air of solemnity or sorrow.

Laugh as we always laughed at the little
    jokes that we enjoyed together.
Play, smile, think of me, pray for me.
Let my name be ever the household word
    that it always was.
Let it be spoken without an effort, without
    the ghost of a shadow upon it.

Life means all that it ever meant.
It is the same as it ever was.
There is absolute and unbroken continuity.
What is this death but a negligible acci-
    dent?

Why should I be out of mind because I am
    out of sight?
I am but waiting for you, for an interval,
somewhere very near,
just round the corner.

All is well.
Nothing is hurt; nothing is lost.
One brief moment and all will be as it was
    before.
How we shall laugh at the trouble of part-
    ing when we meet again!

Introduction

___

BECAUSE GRAMMY AND HUGH TOLD ME TO

It's been two years, one month, thirteen days since my beautiful twenty-year-old son, Hugh, died. And just four hours since I heard from him.

It's my birthday today, and I gave myself the gift of a mediumship reading. The medium, Melissa—the fourth medium I've been to in these two years—so clearly brought Hugh through: describing his high energy, dynamic personality, sense of humor, cause of death, his apology for my pain, and the message that there was nothing I could have done to change the outcome of his passing. There were several gold nuggets of evidence coming through that he was right there, right then, communicating through the medium—a person who connects with and gives voice to those who no longer have a physical form. Melissa asked me, "Is your son really good at getting you to do the things he wants you to do—like, sweet-talking you?"

I laughed. "Yes, he's always been good at getting *every-one* to do what he wants, because he's so charming."

"Well, he's doing that right now," Melissa continued, "and saying, 'Mom, you really need to write a book. It will help people. Be brave.'" Melissa added, "I have the feeling that this isn't the first time you've heard that."

It wasn't. Hugh is not the only one telling me to write a book.

Even before I began writing this story, my maternal grandmother, Grammy—who passed in 2004—told me to, during earlier visits to mediums, when she came through at the beginning of the readings before Hugh did. It went something like this: The medium clearly established that Grammy was present—"There's a woman here who passed in her nineties; she's really smart and well read, good at math and science (Grammy was a junior high school math teacher and one of the few college-educated women in the 1930s), was a very strong woman in a man's world, and she loved nature."

I would respond, "That's my Grammy!"

The medium would then say, "She says you're writing a book."

"No. I'm not writing a book," I'd respond, with a perplexed look on my face.

"Hmmm. She's clearly saying that you're writing a book."

"I'm doing some journaling, but not writing a book." I

didn't resonate with the information coming through, so we moved on.

That happened with other mediums, who said the same thing, noting that my grandmother insisted specifically that I'm writing an autobiography. I adamantly said that I'm not.

My loving, supportive (living) husband—also named Hugh and affectionately referred to as Hughdad in this book—has suggested at times that I write as well. Maybe writing would really help me get through this, he says.

Well, after Grammy repeatedly mentioning that I'm writing a book, and now my son, Hugh, saying that I should, I thought, *Holy cow, maybe I'm supposed to write a book.*

So, here I am, just hours after the mediumship reading.

Since my boy died, I have read so many books, done so much research, watched so many related programs, taken classes, attended online summits and in-person workshops, working passionately to understand: What happens when we die? What is the afterlife? Where is my son, and how can I continue my relationship with him?

The grief that brought me here is different from the grief that brought you here—there are countless manifestations of grief when you've lost someone. It's impacted by the circumstances of their death, how old they were when they passed, what role you played in each other's lives, whether you feel that things were left unsaid, your belief system— so many things. But we are both in pain because we profoundly miss someone.

Even though our circumstances are different from one

another, I hope you can find some way forward in these pages—comfort in knowing that others relate to your grief, that you will survive and even thrive, that joy can coexist with grief. And that the relationship with your loved one continues. Early on, when I was drowning in the quicksand of grief, I was in a fog and couldn't hold my attention well or for very long. The books that resonated most with me had short chapters that I could digest easily and set down until I was ready for another. I write now the way I read then.

I am doing as well as I am now because I found my son. I searched for him, for understanding and proof, and have done the biggest freefall in my life—and I found that he is here in every possible way, except for his body. If I hadn't found him, I don't know where I'd be, if I would still be on this earth, if I would be a functioning person. This whole long, complicated, miraculous journey has led me to know and experience without a doubt that Hugh never left me and is, in fact, closer to me than I could ever imagine, as our relationship continues and we communicate soul to soul. He sees and hears everything, and knows my every thought. And I can communicate with him, with the help of a medium or without, through the many signs he gives me, the thoughts he drops into my mind when I ask. I would never have chosen this path, but it's what I have, and it has given me comfort in the darkest of storms. This book is about my journey with grief and my path to healing through a new kind of relationship with my son in the afterlife.

Before we go one more step together in these pages, I

want you to know that I did not come to my belief in afterlife communication and continued relationships with loved
ones on the Other Side easily or quickly. I don't know if it's
because of growing up with a father who was a psycholo-
gist and a mother who was a counselor—with their focus
on the mind—or because of my college degree in the sciences, or that I work in the tech industry, or if it's just the
way I'm hardwired, but I have a deep questioning need to
understand and to research everything. To connect the
dots of how things are related to one another, not to make
decisions before having all the facts. I couldn't even buy a
clear cross-body bag to take to the Seattle Mariners baseball
stadium without reading all the buyer reviews. So, something as monumental to me as communicating with my son
drenched my research-oriented brain in fuel.

Despite that, I have always had spiritual leanings, an
awareness of something far greater than myself. I grew up in
a family that went to church—casually and open-mindedly—
and I had fun in the church youth group. So, church and the
traditions, hymns, and sacred spaces have always had meaning to me and still do.

But as I've grown older, I've become increasingly disil-
lusioned by the doctrines of some organized religions that
have little to do with a personal relationship with a loving
God—and a love for all creation—but instead have to do
with manifestations of power, because religions are created
and administered by people, who are so human. My spirituality has since grown into a hybrid—one that is less about

religion but has Christian roots and that embraces teachings from Native American spirituality and the mind, body,
and spirit practices of yoga, Reiki, and meditation. And perhaps more than anything, I experience the divine in nature.

Even so and even though, I always pictured a heaven "up
there" and didn't think much about the afterlife. I also want
to say that I have a husband who is open to all possibilities,
but is agnostic and skeptical, and keeps me grounded in this
spiritual quest for knowing.

My journey in the years since Hugh passed has led me
to study mediumship by taking many courses from brilliant mediums and teachers such as Suzanne Giesemann,
Laura Lynne Jackson, James Van Praagh, Michael Mayo,
Marie Manuchehri, Gordon Smith, and tutors at the
Arthur Findlay College located in England, the preeminent
Spiritualist university in the world. I have started to develop
the practices, skills, and sensitivities to be open to communication with those in spirit. In the many practice readings with fellow students and in making a link with their
loved ones, I have seen images playing out like a movie in
my mind. I have heard waterfalls and tap dancing, smelled
metal and perfume, felt their ailments in my body. I saw
clearly the serious-looking grandmother in her brown knee-
length wool coat and sensible shoes, clutching her short-
handled handbag in front of her, and recall just knowing she
was from Eastern Europe, even hearing the word "Ukraine"
when I asked her in my mind where she immigrated from
and seeing her hold up four fingers when I asked how many

children she had. All of which was accurate according to my practice partner. And in another practice reading, having the word "pickles" drop into my mind, which I tried to push away because it was so random, but I had been taught to narrate everything I'm getting because you never know what will have meaning to the living person you're working with. Upon saying to my practice partner, "This is odd, but I'm going to say it anyway—the word 'pickles' just dropped in," I saw her face light up like a marquee as she said, "That's the golden nugget! My mom was famous for her watermelon pickles! The neighbors all waited eagerly when the pickles were ready and it was time for my mom to gift them to all her friends." This was confirmation that I really was connected to her mother.

I don't know where I'll go with this practice, but my research has served to bring me full circle. I'm not just a bereaved mother desperately willing to believe that communication with my son on the Other Side is possible. As I have been able to bring through meaningful spirit communication even in my infancy of development—knowing what that feels like and how it works—I now *know* and *experience* that this is real and true and beautiful and sacred.

This is my story.

1

THE TRAGEDY

I don't want to give much space to the actuality or particulars of Hugh's death. Because it is so excruciating to me, and because it is certainly where this story begins but not what it's about. But this is also a moment that I can't let pass. . . .

Hugh was introduced to "Percs" (street Percocet / oxycodone-acetaminophen / blue M30 pills) at a fraternity party and quickly became addicted, as the vile, wretched opioids do. My husband and I came to suspect an addiction about ten months before Hugh ended up passing, and it was terrifying. At first, Hugh denied that he was using or that he had a problem, but the signs were increasingly clear. After two months of us constantly questioning Hugh, digging into his comings and goings, researching opioid addiction, looking for the telltale constricted pupils, he called me while I happened to be in a doctor's office getting allergy tested. He was in tears and suicidal, confessed his addiction, and begged for help.

What ensued were frantic weeks of trying to get him evaluated and into treatment. Navigating the complex world of insurance coverage and finding availability in good programs that were a right fit meant that his addiction was getting worse and worse while we were scrambling desperately to get him help. He was nineteen—so, an adult—but the adult programs advised, "I wouldn't put him in a program like ours with hardened men who have been using for years." We finally got him into a residential program for young men that *seemed* powerfully transformative for him, then into a step-down program afterward, both of which were great, but we were still seeing the signs. So, we got him into yet a third program, after sleepless nights of trying to get further insurance coverage and documentation of the need.

There was a lot of trauma that our family went through during this time. I don't want to go into it out of respect for Hugh, but we were a family in crisis. Anyone who has experienced addiction with their loved ones knows all too well the devastating impact it has on the entire family. We did everything we could for him. Treatment programs, a substance-abuse counselor, a therapist, a psychiatrist, a doctor, alternative therapies, and so much love and support from family and friends.

It seemed like he was turning a corner. He was seeing exercise as a way to manage the addiction and was getting fit and healthy. We had some great times together as a family. We were hopeful.

On the evening of April 27, 2020, after a particularly wonderful day, he went out for a walk after dinner. There were some things about it that didn't feel right to me, that were a similar pattern to before. And that evening, even though Hugh was really affectionate and particularly engaged, I had a feeling—that intuition—that he'd gone out and bought pills. After he went to his room, I texted him, asking if we could talk. He didn't answer. He must have gone to sleep.

He died in the middle of the night, in his bedroom, just across the hall from our own. We had Narcan—an over-the-counter nasal spray that quickly reverses an opioid overdose—in the hall cabinet that would have saved his life.

He died from fentanyl poisoning. In this horrific opioid crisis, fentanyl is the biggest driver of these accidental drug overdoses. It is a synthetic opioid a hundred times more powerful than morphine and fifty times more powerful than heroin. It is really cheap and highly addictive, and illicit drug manufacturers are making counterfeit pills with it that look exactly like the prescription versions. Anyone buying these pills off the streets is playing Russian roulette with their lives, because the Drug Enforcement Agency (DEA) reports that of fentanyl-laced fake prescription pills analyzed in 2022, six out of ten now contain a potentially lethal dose of fentanyl. Fentanyl is also getting mixed in with other street drugs: marijuana, cocaine, Xanax lookalikes, Adderall lookalikes, heroin—all of it.

I won't tell you what it was like to find my child in the morning, and everything that followed. It is an unfathomable and agonizing experience. The depth of my agony around his death and everything that led up to it is mine, and I don't want anyone else to have it.

2

A MILLION OTHER THINGS

Death by overdose can come to overshadow who a person was before their death. After Hugh's death, I started to feel afraid that he wouldn't be remembered for who he was but by the way he died. It turns out I'm not alone in that fear.

My friend Sue, another bereaved mother who I met on this journey, follows a website called What's Your Grief—a place for grief education, resources, sharing, and support—run by mental health professionals. She sometimes sends me articles that resonate with her. They always resonate with me, too. One was titled: "You Were a Million Other Things."

The author, a grief therapist, explained how and why survivors fear that their loved one's addiction will become their legacy. But the addiction wasn't who they were. They were a million other things. My Hugh certainly was.

He was a firecracker—he loved them, and he was one. He lit up every room he walked into. Life of the party. A Mike and Ike candy fanatic. A sneakerhead. Air Jordans. LeBrons. Vans. Supreme. Canada Goose. Anything high end, really. Joggers and jerseys and flat-billed caps. A snappy dresser. Those beautiful baby blues. Charming. Walking eight dogs at a time. Loved *Modern Family*, every episode. *Family Guy*, same. *Elf*, pretty much anything with Will Ferrell. Watched every James Bond movie in order. Going to the movies and out to eat. ESPN 24-7. Soccer. Football. Basketball, basketball, basketball. Relentlessly dunking in the driveway—annoying the neighbors to no end. Skateboarding in the house. Peeing out the window. Rusting the window hardware. Killing the azalea hedge below. High school Flick game creator. Rap: Chance the Rapper. Mac Miller. Lil Uzi Vert. Kid Cudi. Watershed Music Festival at the Gorge. Singing badly, but don't tell him I said so. Uber Eats. Wasn't fond of red beans and rice, which was weird because he would eat absolutely anything. Rules are just suggestions. Puzzle lover, always had to put in the last piece. "Oh, hell no" to the really trendy slim plaid pants I gave him for Christmas. "I have an idea," said the toddler when negotiating everything. Two-car totaler. Travel bug. Greece. Italy. Iceland's northern lights. Quebec. Hawaii. Alaska. Mexico. Helping build a house for a family in need. Ballard Food Bank volunteer. Happy YMCA Y Guides participant. Risk taker. Confident. Up for any adventure. Supersonic hearer of whispers in another room. Kitten daddy in his dorm room. Goofy, and other people felt safe being goofy around him. Faithful attendee of my dance performances, no matter what. Struggling learner. Had an internal motor that never quit. Complicated. Adoptee— loved and mourned by adoptive and birth families alike. The serious part: People always felt truly seen by him. Community builder. Pulled people in. Helped them belong. Looked out for those who needed an advocate. Intuitive. Emotionally intelligent. Creative thinker. Katy's beau. Friend to so many. Teammate. Student. Coach. Employee. Grandson. Nephew. Cousin. Brother. Son.

I bet many parents think they know their kids better than anyone else knows them. I sure did. Although we maybe do, our kids have a life separate from us, and I learned that we certainly don't know what our kids mean to other people in all those moments we don't see.

After Hugh passed, I ran into one of his preschool teachers on a walk through the neighborhood. She was so sad to hear about Hugh. She had a big tear running down her cheek, and she said, "Hugh was such a beautiful child. He had *so* much life in him—it just radiated out and filled the room." And I thought, "Man, she got that right." Hugh was *always* the energy in the room. He brought the life. He brought the laughs. He was the spark. Even when he was three years old. We always knew that was his superpower.

Then we realized he had another superpower, once we saw him through the eyes of his peers. After he died, many of his friends and acquaintances reached out to tell us stories about Hugh, or posted stories on the digital Kudoboard we set up in memoriam for him, since we couldn't have a memorial service right away because he passed right at the beginning of the catastrophic COVID-19 pandemic and people couldn't gather in groups. There was a similar theme to what people shared about Hugh that I think is beautifully illustrated by this one story:

> A girl from the neighborhood who went to elementary school with Hugh asked if we could meet at nearby Volunteer Park, because she wanted to tell me some stories about Hugh. When she and Hugh were in first grade together, she was struggling socially. The other kids just weren't nice to her. Boys and girls alike teased her. She spent every lunch period in the girls' bathroom—uncertain who to sit with at lunch and who to play with at recess. Hugh somehow picked up on that and invited her to sit at the lunch table with him and his friends. She told him that some of those friends teased her. He said, "We don't have to sit with those guys. We can sit at our own table." And so they did. And other kids started to join them. Then Hugh invited her to play their games on the playground—they were playing war games— and he gave her a role to play. OK, it was as a dog, but still, she had a role. He stood up for

her, and he was so well liked that if he told other people to knock off the teasing, they did. That really broke the ice for this girl. It was very significant. It meant everything to her to come to school every day and know what to do at lunch and recess. She saw this in Hugh throughout elementary school, and said that whenever Hugh saw someone who was picked on or alone, he would go be with them and invite them into his fun world. She and Hugh went to different middle schools, then ended up at the same high school. She said he was that same person then, too.

We've now heard these stories about Hugh through all stages of his life—all the way through to the young men who were in rehab programs with him those last six months. He had so much social and emotional intelligence that he could easily understand what a person needed, what a group needed, what a situation needed. And he understood how to pull people together, how to build community. He loved people so much, and he loved big. At the end of a life, what more would you want people to say about you? We are so proud of our boy and the million beautiful things that he was.

3

SHOWING UP

I have learned so much from our friends and family about how to be there for someone in pain. In the past, I erred on the side of caution and uncertainty in reaching out to people, afraid of saying or doing the wrong thing. Not sure if they wanted to deal with their tragedy privately or publicly. But our people boldly stepped in and are the reason we're still standing today.

From the very beginning, they didn't ask how they could help; they just did something:

- They got up in the wee hours of the morning the day after Hugh died, baked cookies, hopped in the car, and drove across the state to be on our doorstep first thing in the morning.
- They fed us for weeks when we were too numb with shock and grief to manage the day-to-day.

- They sat with us in our backyard, under an old blue tarp in the cold and rain, since it was the early days of the COVID-19 pandemic and we couldn't be together inside.
- They lit our front walkway with twenty luminarias, one for each of Hugh's light-filled years.
- They choreographed and performed a beautiful ceremonial dance in our front yard, which brought me to my knees.
- They started a guys' weekly happy hour outdoors in the cold, but filled with the warmth of support for my husband, Hugh.
- They were a life preserver for Hugh's sibling, Jordan.
- They showed up en masse in our front yard. We couldn't hug, but they lifted us up all the same.
- They rang the doorbell with a book in hand, which ended up being one of the most helpful things I read.
- They brought us flowers and cards, candles, tea, shawls, and other items that wrapped us in comfort.
- They gave us art and jewelry that memorializes Hugh.
- They donated money in Hugh's honor to the Meredith Mathews East Madison YMCA—a place that had so much meaning for Hugh, with basketball leagues, Y Guides, and the pinewood derby.

- And on days that were so dark for me, I would miraculously get texts from ten people checking in to see how I was doing. They knew. They just somehow knew I needed them that day.

They showed up. They kept showing up. And they're still showing up.

4

THE TEXT

What this story is really about started ten days after Hugh's death. Hughdad and I were sitting on the couch on a Friday night, watching TV—numb with shock and grief. I was unable to feel anything in my body, my mind, my emotions. Couldn't smell, couldn't taste. Couldn't concentrate. Couldn't care. Everything moved in slow motion down a one-dimensional plane. When I reflect back on those early days for this writing, it's so painful. Hugh died only once, but when I relive those details, he dies over and over again.

So many things contributed to the fog in those early days. Of course, trauma, pain, and disbelief. And for me, anger also. Hugh was so many magnificent and interesting things, and he was also impulsive and reckless. He made a choice that night—when things were looking up—that destroyed everything. Just look at what he did.

Oh, the horror of it all. Everyone on our street could see

the ambulance and police cars in front of our house that tragic day, and a body bag coming out. We were now *that* family. We had another kid in the house that was our number one priority in the aftermath, and so many things that needed tending to: notifying family and friends, which was excruciating; telling his doctors and therapists, the schools he'd gone to, his sports teams; communicating and arranging with the coroner; and making decisions about Hugh's physical body. It was so overwhelming and unthinkable and exhausting.

So, ten days later, as I sat on that couch in a stupor, my cell phone buzzed with a text message. I had been receiving so many of those as people checked in on me, which was my lifeline. This one was from a colleague at work who I didn't know well, certainly one who didn't know anything about my life, or me about hers. We worked in different departments, and she had my cell number only because she'd organized a carpool to an off-site meeting many months before. Her message said:

Hi Wendy. I don't know if you know this but I'm a psychic and spiritual healer and work with people who have just lost loved ones. If you are open to it, I would like to come over (I'll wear a mask) and help you. I do a guided meditation where I open channels to the angels and have them flood your system with love and healing frequencies. Also, the moment I heard what happened I [felt] angels flying in and [they] showed me a cherry tree, then a cherry pie, then the children's game with cherries. I think this is his sign for you. Anyway, let me know how I can help. You're welcome to call too. I just heard, "I miss her so much" as I'm texting this.

And, please make sure you are getting enough sleep for the next year. It needs to be your number one priority. Call your doctor now if you haven't already. I keep hearing, "I didn't know" over and over again. "I'm sorry and I miss you mom."

Hi. Wow. I would love to talk by phone. When are you available?

She said that she was available right then if I wanted to talk. I told my husband what was up, jumped off the couch, and ran upstairs to our bedroom with the phone, my heart pounding. This woman was not a flake. She was a kick-ass businesswoman who managed a large team. She was a very straight shooter and seemingly logical about everything. Never would I have guessed that she was a psychic and spiritual healer. My brain had trouble computing that connection.

When I called her, she was so graceful about having a conversation with someone who had just lost a child. She said that she's been psychic her entire life. When she heard about Hugh's death—and she had no knowledge of the circumstances—she saw a flurry of angels, which means to her the desire for someone to communicate. I actually don't remember much of our conversation that night; I was just taking in so much of something that came out of the blue. What I really dug my nails into was the text where she said that she heard Hugh say over and over again, "I didn't know. I didn't know. I didn't know. I'm sorry and I miss you, Mom." That resonated with me, because I was certain that Hugh didn't intend to die and that he had no idea those pills were deadly. That really sounded like something he would say about what had happened. Even though I didn't know what to think about everything my colleague was saying, I bought into the idea that a message could come from Hugh somehow.

We talked more about the cherry references that came through and that this was a sign from Hugh. I really didn't know what it meant that cherries were a sign. A sign of what, exactly? She advised me that if ever I think something is a sign from Hugh, it is. We ended the call with her saying that she would be happy to do a spiritual-healing exercise with me if I wanted, and that she would send me the book *Signs* by Laura Lynne Jackson, which she highly recommended.

I recently asked Hughdad what he remembers about the night I had that conversation with my colleague. He remembered that when I came back downstairs and told him about the phone call, my reaction was "Wow, is this possible? Is Hugh trying to communicate?" He recalled that I found the conversation more interesting than bizarre, because I'm predisposed to things of a spiritual nature. He also told me that if a colleague contacted him with a call like this, he would have had a very different reaction and wouldn't have been open to it. When he said that, I realized how much my colleague showed up for me like all our family and friends had. It probably felt risky to her to reach out to me. She had no idea what my beliefs were or how I would take that information. She had no idea how I might then look at her professionally, or if I'd think she was a kook, or if a line would have been crossed. But she did it anyway, and that call was pivotal for me.

In earlier pages of this book, I said that I'm doing as well as I am because I found my son. In actuality, he came for me. When I think about that night, I now realize that Hugh saw a portal, a way to get through to me through someone else— at my most gutted, most vulnerable time, when my defenses were laid bare. I have heard since then from mediums that as much as it was a shock to me that Hugh passed, it was a shock to him as well. I'm sure he wanted to get a message to me that he didn't know the pills he took would end his life. If he were able to see—as I now know he could—the trauma and turmoil he had unleashed on all who loved him, he was unquestionably very sorry.

What I couldn't have possibly known during the phone call that night was that this moment would propel me down the path of a massive spiritual journey that would forever change my life and lead me to a new kind of relationship with my son.

5

I STEPPED IN

After my colleague opened the door during that fateful phone call, I stepped in. Not tentatively, not meekly, but headlong. I was overcome with questions. Even though the things Hugh supposedly said sounded like what he would say, what was all this about cherries and angels? Was this real? And with all respect to the person I worked with but barely knew, how did I know this wasn't just a bunch of crap?

I decided that I wanted to go to a medium. I'm not sure how this even came to me, since mediums were never on my radar. I hadn't thought anything about them and had never spoken to anyone who'd gone to one. As mentioned before, I'm a person who does massive amounts of research before every decision, every trip, every purchase. But I did none of that here—I wanted an appointment with Marie Manuchehri.

I first met Marie sixteen years ago when I was diagnosed

with a breast condition called atypical ductal hyperplasia (ADH), which can increase a woman's chance of getting breast cancer. During the course of my diagnosis and figuring out what to do about it, a friend of mine who had gone through cancer treatments told me that I should go see Marie, an energy healer. Marie is a registered nurse who had worked for years at a Seattle-area hospital in the oncology department. She has an utterly fascinating story about coming from a traditional medical background but, after years of working in the field, suddenly being able to see colors coming off of patients. She was afraid to mention it to anyone out of fear of being sent for a psychiatric evaluation. After a period of time, she confided in her supervisor, who said, "You are seeing energy. Go lay hands on our patients." Marie asked patients who weren't assigned to her if she could lay hands on them—only one ever said no. She touched hundreds of patients over a year's time, during which she moved energy and received information, then would read their chart and compare her intuitive findings with their medical documentation. Through that process, she amassed an encyclopedia of knowledge regarding disease and her intuitive perceptions. The physicians also came to see her as an asset in helping alleviate pain, which she proved to be very proficient at when laying hands on the patients.

Marie eventually left hospital work, set up her own practice, and became highly regarded as an energy healer and a medical intuitive. When I went to see her, she talked about chakras, auras, and how, as I lay on the treatment table, there was a cone coming out of the back of my head that was going all the way down to the building's foundation, which meant I am extremely self-critical (true). But I tell you, during the course of her working with my energy, she told me so many things about my body—past injuries, past ailments, past procedures, current issues—that were absolutely true and that she couldn't possibly have known other than because she has special gifts. She worked to clear blocked energy in my body that can lead to disease, and told me that she didn't see anything tragic in me. What a relief.

But the real point of this story is that during the course of the appointment, she said, "There's someone in the room with us." I said, "Oh, wow, OK." She proceeded to tell me a lot about this man, his approximate height and build, the color of his hair, that he wore dark-rimmed glasses, other things that I didn't connect with. I didn't have many people in my life who had passed at that point, and it didn't sound like either of my grandfathers. Then she said, "It's really interesting; he's got a pocket protector in his shirt pocket with lots of little gadgets in it." I had no idea what that meant or who that might be.

When I got home and told husband Hugh about this, he said, "That sounds like my dad. And because he owned an auto parts store, he always had a pocket protector in his shirt pocket with a tire gauge, grease pencil, small ruler, and all sorts of things in it." I had never met my father-in-law since he passed from cancer before I met my husband, so I didn't know about the pocket protector. At the time, I chalked this up to a really fascinating experience and didn't think anything more about it.

So now—just two weeks after Hugh had passed—when I wanted to see a medium, I thought of Marie. I didn't even know if she really was one, but I had experienced that she was able to see spirits. And I didn't have any idea where to begin with this journey otherwise. I went to her website since I hadn't seen her in many years—and found that mediumship is actually a large part of her practice and that she is now so well known that she's written books, has a call-in radio show and podcast, teaches classes, and is a sought-after speaker. I looked at her online appointment calendar. She was booked out several months, and I was trying to decide what openings worked best with my schedule. I was so disappointed I couldn't get in right away, because I was desperate to explore this and because I'm an immediate-gratification kind of person. When I went to the appointment calendar again a couple of days later, I saw that this time, there was an opening on my birthday that hadn't been there before, so she must have had a cancellation, and it happened to be her earliest available appointment—just a month away. I took that as some kind of sign and snapped it up.

6

ROCKING MY WORLD

Of all the things I've written to this point, this is the passage that gutted me, and found me sitting in front of my computer, weeping. This story right here is the everything in my journey, and I've been avoiding writing about it, unsure of why. I've steered clear, writing many other chapters out of sequence—any other section but this. Now I know why. Not only do I fear not doing its power justice, but this was also my first and most deeply intimate encounter with my son after his death.

I was nervous before the mediumship reading with Marie. So nervous. I knew absolutely nothing of what I know now, nothing about what to expect. I didn't know if this was even a good amount of time after Hugh's passing—six weeks—to go to a medium. Would she be able to connect with him? I was afraid that I would leave disappointed and that it couldn't possibly meet my extraordinarily high

expectations. All I knew was that I trusted Marie, since I'd
had a meaningful experience with her in the past. And that
I was desperately in grief and missing my boy.

The appointment was held over Zoom due to it being the
early days of the pandemic, and no one was holding appointments in person. When I saw Marie years ago for health reasons, it was in person, since she also lives in the Seattle area.
How could this communication with a loved one "across the
veil" possibly work with Marie and me looking at each other
over a computer? I was also feeling stressed that maybe the
technology wouldn't work and that I wouldn't be able to get
into the Zoom room. I had done little videoconferencing up
to that point. My expectations and my worry were through
the roof. I was a mess.

Marie has a beautifully upbeat personality, big smile,
chipper voice, sparkly eyes. She really put me at ease, just as
she had years before. She said that she was going to record
our Zoom session and send it to me, which I was relieved
about. I am an obsessive notetaker, and I knew that if I was
hell bent on taking notes, I might miss being truly present
for even one precious word that could mean everything
to me.

She read *me* first and found me to be in good health, but
with a slight leak in my second chakra. She said that the second chakra is the center of joy, creativity, and sexuality. Not
a shock that I'd have a leak in my joy chakra. She also said
that I was curious about and wanting to pursue something,
and that I have a huge connection to the Divine.

As Marie attuned to spirit for the reading, she first saw a woman present, with gray hair and light gray or hazel eyes. Medium build. Loved the outdoors, was a voracious reader, really smart. She was in a nightgown, which indicated to Marie that she died at home or in hospice, not in a hospital, since she wasn't wearing a hospital gown. I actually didn't know who this person was initially. I now know it was Grammy, making her first appearance, but I couldn't remember where she died and hadn't yet rediscovered her life story, which she had written for the family, where it was so very clear that she dearly loved the outdoors and was a huge reader.

But honestly, I was impatient to move on from this woman whom I wasn't clear about, and get on to Hugh. Very quickly after that, Marie identified a young male coming through, and knew it was my son without any input from me. My heart was beating so fast that I could hear it. *Here we go.*

She asked me how long ago he passed. When I told her six weeks, she said, "Did you have a foretelling that he may leave the earth before you? I have found myself often in the position of reading for parents, and your energy is calmer than any other parent who lost a child this recently. I've never actually asked that of a parent before."

Yes, husband Hugh and I had acknowledged to each other that Hugh's addiction, and his impulsivity and recklessness, could lead to this outcome. And we were terrified of the possibility, constantly in a state of worry, having had a couple of scary episodes with Hugh in recent months where he was doing what we now know is the "death rattle,"—a sign of terminal respiratory failure—while "sleeping" on the couch. Marie said that Hugh was surrounded by dark energy, which meant to her that he'd passed from a tragedy, something unexpected. She also said there was a chemical imbalance in his brain when he was in his body.

The information was all flowing quickly, and she painted the picture of a very social, tall young man with his hair parted on one side and whisked across his forehead—and a big personality. Large hands. "He could have been a ball player." *Oh my, yes, that's him.*

"He knows he's attractive. He says, 'Yeah, I am, and people have been telling me that my whole life.'" Omg, Marie was having a full-on conversation with Hugh, and every bit of it was accurate—including his personality, which never lacked confidence. "He's smart, creative, and complicated." She further described him as really messy, which sealed the deal for me—you just wouldn't believe the chaos of the spaces he occupied. Hurricane Hugh, we called him.

I've since learned that this is called evidence-based mediumship, where there is highly specific information coming through that makes you certain of who the medium is connecting to. It leaves little room for doubt. It's important to establish that evidence before bringing any messages through, which is really where the healing begins. You know for certain that the message is, indeed, coming from your loved one.

"He says his death is his fault, and he didn't intend to leave his body, but how would people know, because, he says, 'I was precarious.' It was an accident, but he takes full responsibility. 'I love you more and more each day,' Hugh says. 'You put up with a lot. You didn't break my spirit, but you were honest with me. I did enough to drive you crazy.'" I felt such a relief in me, and an affirmation that it was an accident, which I had already felt certain about at the time of his passing. I was also happy that he could see, reflect on, and be grateful for my parenting.

Marie said that she wasn't sure why, but Hugh was showing her—like a movie—something that happened with a young member of her family getting arrested as a minor for driving under the influence of alcohol. That person was below the legal limit but shouldn't have had any alcohol in their system since they were a minor. They had to hire an expensive lawyer to keep it off their record. That's the *exact* scenario of something that happened with Hugh after a high school graduation party, and what we had to do after Hugh was eventually charged with reckless driving. When I told Marie about that, she said that spirits will often show her something in her own life that relates, so that she knows what to convey. This was another bit of evidence in the story of the reading.

Hugh was apparently very busy during the reading. Marie said that initially, he was standing next to my left shoulder, and that he'd leaned down and kissed me on the cheek, which I didn't feel. At some point, he brought me a huge wooden bowl filled with many different kinds of beautiful, colorful fresh fruit. Marie thought he was telling me that I needed to eat better. That point was well taken, as I hadn't been eating consistently, or the healthiest. I was just filling my body with whatever, because I didn't have much appetite. And then later in the reading, he was planting a field of the darkest purple lilacs behind me. Neither Marie nor I knew the significance of that. Afterward, I searched online for the significance of lilacs. They are said to be a sign of new life because they are one of the first flowers to bloom every spring—earth's way of letting us know we survived winter. Each color of lilac holds different meanings, and dark purple is said to symbolize a connection to the spiritual realm, and that someone is concerned about or knows about spiritual mysteries. That was very meaningful to me and could apply to Hugh, me, or both of us.

Marie reported that Hugh saw all the outpouring after his passing. At first, he was embarrassed, because he didn't realize how much people liked him, but he shouldn't have been surprised. He knew he was popular. It was all too overwhelming, and he had to turn his back. "He will be at his memorial. There will be so many people there."

We'd delayed his memorial because of the pandemic and the inability for people to gather in large numbers. We had asked his friends if we should try to do a virtual service or wait and do it in person. They said that we absolutely needed to wait until everyone could be together. It was the right move, but this was another very difficult thing for us, as it was for the millions of people who lost someone during the pandemic. And yes, there were so many people at Hugh's eventual service—a year and eight months later due to continuous surges and new variants of the COVID-19 virus.

I told Marie that I felt so bad for Hugh because he had pretty severe ADHD, which made his life hard. He didn't ask for it. It wasn't his fault. It was the lot he'd been given. And it made school and jobs and navigating life difficult for him.

Marie said, "Hugh liked who he was. His impulsivity and big personality made him unique. He liked his life and thought it was fun. You don't need to feel sorry for him. He figured out how to maneuver school and sees himself as part of the change that needs to happen in education and other organizations. He doesn't want you to feel sorry for him. The only regret he has is that you're in so much pain."

Through Marie, Hugh said, "I would never, ever have wanted you to be in this much pain. That's the one thing I didn't compute. I can see my selfishness, and I am eternally sorry for that."

Marie continued, "Hugh can read your mind. He has the full vision of your life. He loves this conversation, because he wants more than ever to continue a relationship with you."

His parting messages to me were that he was grateful I was somewhat prepared for this. "He loves you so, so much and is incredibly sorry for the pain he caused you, your family, and his friends."

And then the sixty minutes were up. A precious, priceless, lifesaving hour. An hour that rocked my world and challenged what I believed. A sacred hour with my son that I would never have imagined possible.

If I were a different person, that reading with Marie could have been a one-and-done. It was incredible, wasn't it? That could have been the end of my story, because I would have walked away knowing that my son is *here*, that there is consciousness after death, that communication and the relationship continue, that Hugh takes responsibility for his death and is so very sorry for the pain he caused, that he knows my every thought and action. What a profound and life-changing gift that knowledge is.

Although the reading ultimately left me feeling stunned, elated, and hopeful that there is something so much more in life and after life, I was also profoundly heartbroken that this was now the state of my relationship with my son.

I could have walked forward with that, with joy mixed in with the pain of my heart. I now know plenty of people who have had some sort of spiritual experience with a loved one and feel more at peace and can just feel comfort knowing the presence of the loved one in their life.

But I am me, and instead, it was just the beginning of my journey.

7

THERAPY

After I saw Marie and experienced the undeniable presence of Hugh, I felt a powerful desire to learn more about how mediumship works, but I was stalled for a number of reasons. For starters, work had become incredibly demanding.

After Hugh died, I took a whole nine f*cking days off work. I could have taken much more time off—I had twelve weeks of sick leave that I hadn't used, and this was certainly a situation in need of sick leave. But, I didn't know what else to do. *I did not know what else to do* besides go back to work.

Work had actually been a haven for me over years of challenges with Hugh and his sibling. They both had difficulties with learning differences and various diagnoses, and with Hugh's ADHD, I was on every teacher's speed dial. I spent every spare moment scheduling appointments with specialists and researching programs that could be helpful. Work was so good for me because I could go into the office and put my imaginary Cap of Hardship on a shelf and immerse myself in the day-to-day workings of a job I enjoyed, with colleagues that I adored. Head down, thinking about something else, being productive. Then, at the end of the day, the cap would go back on, and I'd head home.

Yet again, work saved me after Hugh died. Unfortunately, the pandemic hit my workplace hard financially. I wasn't furloughed, but people I supervised were, and I had to do their jobs as well as mine. And at the same time, my boss decided to retire, so I was also filling in on some of her responsibilities. I had so much work to do that I *had* to get up every day, put one foot in front of the other, and be a highly functioning professional. Without that responsibility, I think I would have been curled up in a dark corner.

Really, the most significant reason why I wasn't able to delve into mediumship after encountering Hugh during my reading with Marie was because I had just experienced a terrible, terrible trauma. Every day felt like a monumental task to get through. Sleeplessness, loss of appetite, difficulty concentrating, anxiety, hopelessness, low energy. Grief can be serious business.

I barely had the bandwidth to get out of bed, show up for work, and keep myself fed and presentable. In those early months, as much as I would have liked to have learned more about mediumship and the possibility of Hugh's afterlife, I knew I first needed the support of a mental health specialist to right my ship. Thankfully, I already had a relationship with a terrific therapist, Lindsey, who I'd been seeing over the past few years even before Hugh died. Lindsey was immensely helpful to me through the challenging times our family went through while Hugh was spiraling into addiction. And when Hugh died, I don't know what I would have done without her.

I highly recommend having a neutral and trained party to whom you can say what's deepest, darkest, and most hopeless in your heart. I was trying to be strong and put on a brave face for everyone else. With Lindsey, I didn't have to. I remember telling her in one session that it felt like I was wearing a big sign on my chest or a badge of some kind that announced to the world, wherever I went, that I was a mother who lost a child. For those who know me, is that the first thing they now see every time they see me—first and foremost—that I've lost a child? Does it ever *not* cross their mind and color their lens? Even when we see each other often and laugh and do fun things, do they not first see a woman with an unthinkable tragedy?

Lindsey took me through a very helpful exercise called Lifespan Integration, which is a protocol to clear or heal grief and trauma. It utilizes repetition of a timeline to clear past trauma and relies on the body and mind to innately heal itself. I share it here for anyone who might benefit from this powerful exercise. Apparently, in trauma, it's common for people to have disjointed memories, and the brain works hard to try to fit the story together. In this exercise, by putting the story together, the brain can relax, integrate, and move toward healing. It also shows people that they have survived their past and are living here and now. Lindsey had me start wherever I wanted in the story of Hugh's death and recount every memory that came to me. I started with Hugh coming back home after his freshman year of college and the beginning of the Troubles with drugs. I told the story through his passing and everything afterward and how I was doing in the present day. We worked on that story for weeks, with the opportunity for me to go back over the story and include additional memories, additional feelings, additional realizations. Lindsey wrote it all out by hand.

Once I felt that I had the story all down, Lindsey read it back to me—over and over again, through several sessions, to lock that into my being. I could see the point that once I had the entire traumatic story down, my brain didn't have to recreate it, fill in the blanks, or search for the threads of understanding. The repetitions integrate past experiences and prove to your body-mind system that time has passed. Lindsey typed up the story and gave it to me. I've made further additions to the point where I feel it is complete. I actually treasure having the whole thing on paper, because I'm afraid of forgetting—anything. Even the hard stuff. Because every memory ties me to my boy.

The other purpose my work with Lindsey served was to keep me grounded in the here and now, in the material world, as I was about to embark on a life-changing spiritual journey, which I'm eager to get back to here.

8

CHERRIES

About three months after Hugh died, my colleague finally mailed me the book *Signs: The Secret Language of the Universe* by Laura Lynne Jackson, which she'd offered to share with me the night of our fateful phone call. She apologized for the delay, but like me, she had been buried in the pandemic chaos at work and was just now coming up for air.

I was so hungry to read the book after checking out the stellar reviews—which, of course, I researched—and when it finally arrived, I devoured it whole. It lived up to the hype. Laura Lynne is a world-renowned medium. I had never heard of her beforehand, but I hadn't had any reason to, I guess. She's actually a really big deal in that world and was featured in another *New York Times* bestseller by investigative journalist Leslie Kean—*Surviving Death: A Journalist Investigates Evidence for an Afterlife*—which was then made into a Netflix docuseries also featuring Laura Lynne.

At the beginning of *Signs*, Laura Lynne posed some questions that grabbed me.

"What if, when we take a long, mindful look at everything around us, we're not actually seeing everything? What if we're only seeing part of what's really there? What if we are missing an entire layer of reality?

"And what if, by simply opening our hearts and our minds to a new vocabulary of seeing and understanding, we begin to see a much bigger picture? What if the world suddenly becomes a magnificent tapestry of connections and signs and light and love, all woven into the ordinary fabric of life that we're so used to?"

With chapter titles like "Cereal in the Car," "1379," and "Ghost Calls," the book is filled with compelling stories from Laura Lynne's own life and of people she has done readings for who have received remarkable signs and unexplained synchronicities from their loved ones—from the pay-off of a purple elephant that was specifically requested as a sign, or the Raggedy Ann doll, or the soda bread that snagged the attention of the bereaved and had tremendous meaning.

Laura Lynne says that our loved ones are trying really, really hard to send us messages and signs—hitting us over the head with them, really—but we miss them. Even really big, bold, great signs. We're distracted by our minds, our phones, our lives. We might even walk right by them and see them, but not really *see* them. And we think, *I never get any signs from my loved one.*

I was starting to feel excited about the possibility that Hugh might be trying to speak to me through sending me signs. How amazing that this communication was possible. But I also felt deflated, because like so many people, I indeed said "I never get any signs" to myself when reading Laura Lynne's words. But had I?

Two months after Hugh passed, Hughdad and I started taking long weekends away with Jordan to just get the hell out of Dodge. The pandemic had everyone cooped up and a bit hopeless, and 24-7 in this house where Hugh died was smothering us.

The first trip—before I even read *Signs*—was to a house in Oregon that I booked on a vacation rental site. In my typical modus operandi, I looked into twelve different properties in the area, trying to find just the right one, and settled on one with a hot tub and air-conditioning (both very important to Jordan) and on a golf course (it must be very pretty). The website doesn't give you the address until you've booked and your trip is coming up, then they give you the address and the directions. The address was 2 Cherrywood Lane.

The "cherry" part snagged me. I thought back to that conversation I'd had with my colleague just ten days after Hugh passed, when she said that she thought cherries were going to be a sign for me because she had seen a cherry tree, a cherry pie, and the children's game Hi Ho! Cherry-O in her vision—and none of them had meaning to me other than they all had the word "cherry." And things with the word "cherry" just didn't cross my path often. I thought, *Huh, well I wonder if this is part of the cherry sign.* But then as soon as the thought came, I doubted it.

We had a nice enough time away, although we were aching for Hugh's presence and despondent over the reality of our new life without him. He was just two and a half months gone. It felt like we were fake enjoying it. And it felt so wrong to have any fun or to laugh.

Even so, we decided to book another getaway up in northern Washington on beautiful Puget Sound two months later. The address had nothing to do with cherries, but as we turned onto the road of the rental, there was a huge billboard that said "Welcome to Cherry Point. Home of the Cherry Point Aquatic Reserve." Snagged me again. I had no inkling about this being a part of the area where we would be staying. By this time, I had read *Signs.* Maybe cherries *were* a sign.

And a couple of months after that, the third place we went to was on the Washington side of the Columbia River, which divides Washington and Oregon. We stayed up in the high prairie over the river. After we arrived, moved our bags and food in, and got settled, I went into the kitchen to get a glass of water. I opened up the cabinet where the glasses were stored and was met with shelf paper lining all the shelves—covered in a print of cherries.

I reflected back on Laura Lynne's book and thought to myself, *OK. I think I get it.* Hugh was giving us signs that he was there with us on our travels. He goes where we go. He is not tied to our house or to Seattle, or to any space or time. Where we go, there he is. We were all missing him, yet he was telling us he was there with us all along. This was my first introduction to signs from Hugh. And it took having someone else tell me what to look for.

I've read that some people receive a sign right away from their loved one that they are OK on the Other Side. I wished I had received one from Hugh. But now, as I opened my mind to seeing what was right in front of me all along, I realized that I *had* gotten a sign from Hugh. The night he died, I was sitting by him at dinner. I glanced over and saw him looking at his bank account on his phone. I questioned him about that because I thought it was weird. He hadn't worked for months and didn't have any money. Why would he be checking his bank account? He said that someone owed him money and had paid up. It was after dinner that he went for the walk, and I just had a bad feeling about it.

After the horrors of the next morning—after the police left, after the ambulance left with Hugh's body in it, after the city fire department chaplain left and the three of us were left in the silence of cataclysmic loss—I felt compelled to check Hugh's bank account, which I had access to. Sure enough, he'd had a deposit the day before, and a withdrawal that evening. And the balance in his account was now $7.77. Multiples of seven appear throughout the Bible and are often associated with God, Divine guidance, and spiritual perfection. The number 777 is associated with God, and it triumphs over the devil's 666. I realize now that it was an extraordinarily clear sign, and a great gift, showing me that Hugh was OK. He was with God.

This was really something—to be opened up to the idea that Hugh can, and is, speaking to me through signs. That communication is possible. That I don't have to go to a medium to hear from him. This started to give me the first sparks of hope, of comfort, that perhaps all was not lost.

9

THE YEAR OF SURVIVAL

As anyone who has lost a child or someone much loved knows, surviving the first year is tough—for me, the toughest. I call this time the Year of Survival.

The biggest goal was to get through all the "firsts": the first Mother's Day and Father's Day without Hugh, Thanksgiving, Hugh's birthday, our birthdays, Christmas, New Year's, the first anniversary of Hugh's passing, which we call his angel date. I told myself that putting so much dread into those firsts was just a human construct—my mind putting more meaning into the date than necessary. But it's real. Those milestone days are of mental, emotional, physical, and spiritual significance, and the heartache couldn't be denied. We were really blessed to have so many of our people checking in with us on those days.

I kept up with my therapy, kept doing my job, and I did a lot of reading on the topics of grief, healing, and the afterlife.

The session with Marie had sparked in me a keen desire to understand more clearly everything that had happened and had been said during the session. But I had no time or energy for anything except reading, and even that was scattershot because I struggled to concentrate.

But during this time, I was learning to trust that Hugh was really here. From the reading with Marie, to the cherries, to other signs I'd received of Hugh's presence, I was starting to take in the idea that the Other Side, and Hugh, are actually right here, right now—not "up there" somewhere, where we would reunite some day when I also pass.

After reading *Signs* and following one of Laura Lynne's suggestions of asking our loved ones for a sign that is seemingly difficult to fulfill and watching it still magically unfold, I received a really special sign from Hugh that was another confirmation of his presence. In the book, Laura Lynne says that she herself asked her father for the sign of a purple elephant. You might think, *How will that ever come to fruition?* But it did for her in a really fun way.

When I wanted to ask Hugh for a difficult-to-fulfill sign, I couldn't think of anything creative, so I decided to ask him for a purple elephant, too. Not long after, I went for a walk in a neighborhood I hadn't been in before and found a road that took me past the backyards of some waterfront homes. After walking about fifteen minutes, I glanced over at one of the yards, and behind a low fence, I saw a huge metal elephant sculpture in the grass. *Wow, that's weird. Why would someone have a huge metal sculpture of an elephant in their backyard? That is so random.* It wasn't purple, though—it was just a silver metal. But then, I realized that my view of the sculpture was partially obscured—by a large dark-purple lilac bush, similar to what Hugh was apparently planting behind me in the reading with Marie. I was looking at the elephant through a purple veil. That stopped me short. I lingered there for a long time and soaked that up. Laura Lynne's book was definitely opening me up to the magnificent tapestry of connections and signs.

Signs is more than just a book about beautiful stories of continued connections. She talks about how quantum physics shows us that all matter is energy, which leads us to the conclusion that we, also, are made of energy—we emit energy, and we affect each other with our energy. The more we shift our energy into the positive, the more open we become to all things, including signs from the Other Side, and she offers guidance for how to do that. She also talks about the importance of surrender. Of letting go. That continues to be my number one lesson to learn. I just got the truth shivers flooding my body as I write this. So yes, that is definitely my primary lesson to learn.

Her first book, which I read second, is also a *New York Times* bestseller: *The Light Between Us: Stories from Heaven. Lessons for the Living.* This book tells the fascinating story of her growing to understand her unique gifts—from hiding them and being a high school English teacher by day and a medium by night, to embracing her gifts and using them for the powerful healing that mediumship can bring to those in grief. The story opens with her on her way to do a group reading for bereaved parents at the Forever Family Foundation in New York. As she was driving on the turnpike from her home, her car became crowded with the spirits of the children, with their stories and pleas pouring out:

"Tell them I am still here," one said.

"Tell them I am still part of their lives," said another.

"Tell them, 'I love you and I see everything that goes on.'"

"Please don't cry for me. I'm okay."

"I am not dead. I am still your child."

"Don't think of me as gone. I am not gone."

"Please tell them I'm not gone!"

I read this page over and over. And over and over. *I am not gone. I am not dead. I see everything that goes on. I am still here.* This gave me indescribable comfort that Hugh is also all those things. And it sparked in me the colossal hunger to understand the afterlife, afterlife communication, mediumship, and how it works.

I became a huge fan of Laura Lynne. Around the time of Hugh's first angel date in April, I signed up for Laura Lynne's three-day retreat at the Omega Institute in New York called An Illuminated Life: Opening to the Secret Language of the Universe. It was going to be held in late September, five months later. It seemed a miracle that I got a spot because it filled up immediately.

Meanwhile, I was still working at a ridiculously stressful job with extreme hours. What once had been a distraction and refuge from the grief and suffering I was slogging through had now become a significant health hazard. I was just a shell of a person, so burned out. I had no choice but to leave my job to heal my entire being from burnout and to find another way to handle my grief. I needed to take stock of every aspect of my life and turn serious attention to myself. It was the end of an era for me. And the beginning of something much bigger.

The retreat seemed to be the placeholder for a new beginning in my life and my healing journey. I made all the flight, hotel, train, and shuttle arrangements, figuring out the puzzle of how to get to the remote institute in the beautiful Hudson Valley of New York. I put all my wishes, hopes, and anticipation into this retreat. Then, just three weeks before it was to be held, the entire event was canceled. It was the fall of 2021, and due to a major uptick of the Delta variant of COVID-19 across the United States, everything was getting shut down. Again. I was *crushed*. Crushed.

This was the first real action I had taken on my journey to start a deeper dive and to find a new relationship with my son and my grief. How could I feel so led to this, so right about it, to have so many things fall into place to allow me to go, only to have the rug pulled out from under me? I hit the floor hard.

10

THE SHIFT

In my massive disappointment over the cancellation of Laura Lynne Jackson's retreat, just a couple days later, the Universe did what I now understand it does—it fed me an ad. When scrolling through Instagram. Or when ordering face masks online. I don't know what I was doing at the time, but somehow when I wasn't looking for it, there it was, a sign. Beyond the Veil: The Science & Mysteries of Near-Death Experiences, Crossing Over & the Afterlife—a weeklong, fully online summit offered through the Shift Network, which was going to happen at the exact time I would have been at the retreat. Six speakers per day for five days. And I was completely available after having just quit my job two months before with the intention of taking as much as a year off before looking for another job. This became the opportunity for my deep, deep dive—coming up on a year and a half after Hugh passed.

I had never heard of the Shift Network. The founders of the Shift Network believe it will take "millions of awake, connected, and inspired individuals to collaborate on the changes that are needed for our world to truly shift." Their ultimate aim is to help people grow and awaken in order to cocreate a world that is just, sustainable, healthy, and peaceful. This really spoke to me not only in terms of the spiritual awakening I was starting to experience but also because of the enhanced global view I had during the pandemic. For once, everyone in the world had a common enemy, the COVID-19 virus. We needed each other. We affected each other. It was going to take all of us and our vigilance to beat this thing. Sadly, it wasn't as unifying as I'd hoped it would be, and actually became polarizing, but can't we somehow cocreate a world that is better for all of us?

The network has hundreds of faculty members teaching a vast array of courses, from raising conscious kids to health and wellness, shamanism, healing practices, medical intuition, and mediumship. This summit—and being exposed to the thirty different topics surrounding the afterlife—was truly the shift that took me down the path of inquiry, discovery, and research, which brought me back to a relationship with my son.

Spoiler alert: I did make it to Laura Lynne's retreat a year later, and it was glorious. After attending this online summit, though, I eventually came to realize that it was likely more beneficial that I went to the summit than the retreat at that time in my journey because I was introduced to far more than mediumship. It gave me a broad—and extremely comforting and exhilarating—view of what happens when we die, our soul's path, the afterlife, and healing. All the sessions were terrific, but two had me riveted and charted my trajectory. In a session called "A Hundred Little Deaths Before Dying," Stephen Jenkinson, who has master's degrees from Harvard University (theology) and the University of Toronto (social work)—and is the author of the award-winning book *Die Wise: A Manifesto for Sanity and Soul*—talked about his extensive work with dying people in hospice services and their families. He described in detail the business of dying, but this was what grabbed me:

> "Let's not diminish the fact that a lot of people are more than a little concerned about what becomes of them, corporeally and spiritually and so on after they die. But I found in my time in the death trade, I was honestly shocked to learn that came a distant second to something that was rarely articulated, rarely broke the surface, but was always sort of agitating just below the surface and throwing everybody terribly off the scent of trying to die in some kind of sane way. That was, in a phrase, what the rest of us will do with them after they die. . . . They were less than assured that the rest of us would see to it that they had a place of esteem and

consequence among us after they died. They were no longer willing to count on that in some fundamental way."

So, I took from this session that perhaps more than anything else, we're afraid of being forgotten—and not continuing to matter—after we die. That pulled hard at me, as I've considered that for myself sometimes and have wondered if I will pass unnoticed from this life as just a regular person living a quiet existence. What have I mattered?

That was a huge moment for me, and ultimately for Hughdad. After that session, I spoke with him about how we could do more to make sure Hugh was honored and not forgotten. We decided to purchase an urn space for his ashes at our local cemetery with his name and dates engraved in beautiful, permanent granite—proof that he walked this earth. And most importantly, we decided we wanted to create a charitable fund or foundation in his name. It started a dynamic conversation between us as we explored what kind of good work we could do in the community. We wanted it to be something Hugh was passionate about and that would keep his name out there. We certainly didn't figure it all out in that weekend, but it galvanized us in a powerful way.

The other pivotal session for me was "No More Fear: Mediumship and the Ultimate Freedom" with Suzanne Giesemann. Suzanne, a messenger of hope if ever there was one, is one of the most influential spiritual leaders of our time—and one of the most unlikely. She is a former US

Navy commander and commanding officer, and served as aide to the chairman of the Joint Chiefs of Staff during 9/11. Disciplined, regimented, and highly structured, never in the proverbial million years would she have envisioned mediumship skills unfolding in herself after the passing of her beloved stepdaughter Susan. Susan, a sergeant in the US Marine Corps, and her unborn baby were struck and killed by lightning as Susan crossed the flight line where she was stationed.

This life- and perspective-changing event opened in Suzanne the abilities and interest in becoming a medium. She is now one of the preeminent evidential mediums in the world. I love a quote I later saw from Suzanne's husband, Ty, a retired US Navy captain, who has gamely supported her on this extraordinarily unexpected career change, saying, "I married a naval officer, not a medium." But here they are.

In Suzanne's session, two things ended up meaning everything to me:

One, in talking about Susan's passing, she mentioned the nonprofit organization called Helping Parents Heal (HPH), which provides support and resources for parents who have experienced the passing of a child—and said she is a big supporter of the group. She appreciates that every person in the group is on a similar journey, and upon being introduced to other parents who experience deep grief and loss, they become aware that their children are still part of their lives. They hear from other parents who have had readings with mediums or who talk about the incredible signs and evidence their children send to show they are still here. The parents often start meditating so they can have their own connection with their child. Suzanne said, "It's a process for those of us left behind, to come to know that death is not the end."

I hadn't come across Helping Parents Heal in my inquiries into grief groups. I had never heard of it, which actually surprises me now that I know how highly regarded the organization is and that it has an international presence. I think my online searches at the time were around "grief groups, Seattle" or "grief support near me, after the death of a child." I thought that, of course, I would want to attend a group in person. But there was none of that happening anyway during the pandemic, and I was thinking too small. Helping Parents Heal was incredibly adept at turning all their meaningful support online and had brilliant programs during the pandemic. After Suzanne talked about the group a bit, I thought that this was exactly what I was looking for. It sounded like these could be my people, and I couldn't wait to look into it and get involved.

Secondly, Suzanne talked about courses she offers through the Shift Network—courses to help people connect with their loved ones on the Other Side by learning mediumship skills. She said, "We're talking about taking away the fear of death. Grief is another whole process. Still, in either case, grief or fear, knowing that we can still contact those who have crossed the veil really makes a big difference." What she enjoys doing is teaching people tools to contact loved ones themselves. What? This is a learned thing? I had certainly started recognizing the signs Hugh was sending me, but I, just a regular person, could learn how to connect with him? This was all starting to change my ideas about the finality of death, and what that meant about Hugh and our relationship, and for myself. This was really exciting and seemed a perfect dovetail to my grief journey.

Sign me up. For Suzanne's courses and for Helping Parents Heal.

11

SOUL-TO-SOUL COMMUNICATION

It took less than twenty-four hours for me to decide to sign up for Suzanne Giesemann's seven-week online course called Expand Your Innate Mediumship Skills with Soul-to-Soul Communication. It was available on demand. The beauty of that is I was able to start this course just ten days after the summit, after being exposed to Suzanne and finding her course on the Shift Network's site.

I'd heard the terms "the Other Side," "Beyond the Veil," and "Crossing Over." What does it all mean? As I dug into it, I learned that the terms are all really synonymous with the afterlife—which some people call life after death. Some call it life after life. Some call it survival of consciousness. Some call it Heaven. But what is the veil that is crossed? *Where* is the Other Side? I have heard as many explanations as teachers, books, and research that I've accessed.

Laura Lynne Jackson describes a veil between the living and those in spirit so thin and transparent that it's like our loved ones being on one side of a sheet of paper and us being on the other. When we hold the paper, we can see and hear and access the other side easily, and we're actually touching both sides. The other side of the paper is right there. That's how close they are to us. Some mediums say the veil is just a vibrational shift that separates us.

In Suzanne Giesemann's course, she told us the body is the veil. It's a box that defines our awareness, and when we shed it, we have *complete* awareness, she said. Our brain is critical to our day-to-day living: It's what helps us drive a car safely, manage projects in our jobs, and get what we need at the grocery store. But it is a powerful filter, so caught up in the story of ourselves and the realities we create, that it doesn't listen well. It misses the signs and messages from our loved ones, from the far bigger picture, from our universal connectedness. Once we are freed from our bodies, everything else about us is still right here: our consciousness, intelligence, personality, interests, memories, and now *universal* awareness. The only difference between what and who we are before and after death is the human mind and body, made up of trillions of cells, each with its own energy, so busy and so distracting.

I found resonance with all the explanations I was learning. They all showed me that our loved ones are not anywhere but here. The more I studied mediumship with Suzanne and ultimately other teachers, the less concerned I became about the terminology or what it really means.

What started to matter more was receiving unequivocal evidence that Hugh was here, that he could hear me, see me, and know my life. And above all else, this is what started to transform my relationship with grief.

Suzanne talked passionately about Heavenly love: the love of the Divine, or God, or Source, or Great Spirit. She called that entity Joy. Joy has the deepest, unending, unconditional, profound love for each of us. Our soul is the aspect of us that is eternal and aligned with all that is the divine: kindness, compassion, love. We are all part of one interconnected web, and we feel most joyful when in alignment with our soul and our true nature. All communication we have with our loved ones or guides is soul to soul, and we must have patience with receiving communication, as it will happen in our soul's course.

Five months after I finished the first course with Suzanne, I signed up for her course Holistic Mediumship. This time, the course was offered online in real time with 720 eager participants.

Suzanne offered us a lot of guidance and practices for connecting with our loved ones beyond the veil. I actually had a hard time remembering all the steps represented by the many catchy acronyms she had for the practices—acronyms being staples of her military training. But there was also so much easy, practical guidance:

- Intention. Intention. Intention. To connect with our loved one. That's key. We don't really have to *do* anything, but like a radio, we need to get on the right channel to communicate, and that happens through intention.

- It's easier to get on the right channel if you raise your vibration. Feeling grateful, joyful even, brings our vibration up closer to where our loved ones are, freed from their bodies and basking in Joy.
- Surrender your ego, your human story, your expectations, and just be present.
- Suzanne embraces hemi-sync music, which is based on research that different sound patterns engage both hemispheres of the brain and lead to different levels of consciousness. She has recorded several hemi-sync meditations that are available, as well as so many of her teachings and resources. She is so generous with her knowledge and wants all to benefit.

This only touches the tip of the proverbial iceberg—the many hours of classroom time, reference videos, and practice with other classmates.

There's an exercise she taught us called automatic writing that many spiritual teachers recommend to people, to access wisdom from your spirit guides or your Higher Self, or to communicate with your loved ones across the veil. Which realm you access is dependent on your intention and who you want to communicate with. Setting an intention is essential when doing any spiritual work and trying to connect in any way.

When I wondered how I could possibly distill all that learning and the influence it had on my journey, I decided to do an automatic-writing session and set the intention to connect with higher wisdom—wherever that comes from—to help me know what to write about. I asked the question, "What will help lead people out of the darkness?" A lot came to me surprisingly quickly as I set pen to paper. What came to my mind: "I know how the readers feel. I understand the unfathomable pain. I'm going on this yearslong journey so they don't have to. I can be a shortcut, if they believe me. How do I become trustworthy in these pages? Be raw, transparent, relatable, data driven, the everyperson. Talk about what I learned about the Universe and the afterlife. What has been most helpful to me? And give helpful exercises."

OK.

Most automatic-writing and meditative practices start with deep breaths to calm and slow the body and the mind. Inhaling is linked to the sympathetic nervous system, which controls the fight-or-flight response, and exhaling is linked to the parasympathetic nervous system, which influences our body's ability to relax. So, for these practices, it is always recommended to exhale longer than you inhale—for instance breathing in for four counts and exhaling for six. Doing that several times has the profound effect of calming us.

If you want to connect with your loved one, you set the

intention of having a special session with them. Let them know the date and time in advance. Create a quiet, sacred space for yourself, perhaps light a candle, have flowers nearby, whatever feels meaningful for you. Prepare yourself with the calming breaths, and focus on something that makes you feel grateful, which has the wonderful effect of raising your vibration and making it easier to connect. Then surrender the story you've made up about yourself and your loved one, and all expectations of how your loved one will communicate.

One method is to tell your loved one that you would like evidence that it is them infused into the conversation. Whether you prefer typing on a computer or putting pen to paper, write a question or two you would like to have answered. It might even be something like "What do I need to know right now?" Remain passive and wait for what happens. Write what you're getting, and write until it doesn't flow anymore. Thank them for the beautiful time together. Don't feel discouraged if you don't get anything, or much. This practice takes practice. I know people who have a regular schedule of doing this and have received some incredible experiences with it.

The automatic-writing exercise I outlined is one of Suzanne's. But the exercise I have since used the most frequently to connect with Hugh, with wonderful experiences, is a meditation that Suzanne also taught us.

It starts in the same way as the writing exercise. After the deep breathing, expressing my gratitude to the Universe to raise my vibration, and setting my intention to connect with Hugh, I will say something like "Hugh, I love and miss you so much. I know you're here, but I still want a sign from you. Please tell me what sign you'll give me in the coming days that shows me you're here and that you hear me." And then I wait. Suzanne instructed us to let our loved one drop in the sign they will give us—apparently they can see into the future and know what they can fulfill.

At first, my brain was always trying to make something up, and I could tell it was coming from me. But over time, with patience, I started to experience that something really random would pop into my mind that I never would have made up. I will always hear a word, and also see it spelled out or get a visual representation. I started writing the word on a sticky note and putting it on the back of my computer monitor so that I would sort of forget about it and not think about it. Each one of those signs has been fulfilled in some beautiful and unexpected way.

My very first one was "green truck." Admittedly, as my first one, I was looking for green trucks everywhere and saw a lot that were *mostly* green—garbage and recycling trucks—and wondered if that was the sign. Until I was at the venue where my family had decided to hold Hugh's celebration of life. We had held off until the situation with the pandemic calmed down enough for us to hold an event in person. I was there to meet with the staff for a walk-through before the event in six weeks. As I was waiting outside for them to unlock the door and let me in, the greenest green truck pulled up right in front of the building. Dark green from bumper to bumper, no color but. And right when I was feeling so tender and emotional because of why I was there.

That was beautiful, but my mind kicked in and I thought, *Was that just a coincidence?* So the signs Hugh dropped in subsequently got a lot more unusual. There have been many great ones, but my favorite sign of all time has been this. As usual, I asked, "Hugh, please tell me what sign you'll give me in the coming days that show me you're here." And I waited.

"Diplo."

Diplo? I heard it and saw it spelled out in my mind. What the hell kind of word is that? How are you going to fulfill that, Hugh? But by now, I had learned to trust, because it always came to be. So, I wrote it on a sticky note and put it on the back of my computer monitor.

A week later, I was driving down the freeway on my way to a doctor's appointment. I heard a song on the radio that I liked and looked over at the digital screen on the console, where it shows the artist and the name of the song playing.

The artist was Diplo. And the song was "Don't Forget My Love."

I was in disbelief. I pulled the car over. And I cried grateful tears.

I later googled the song lyrics, and I love the line "Breathe me in just so you can feel me with you even when I'm not around." I so cherish that sign from Hugh.

I also love the time I had both "gladiator" and "gladiolus" pop into my mind at the same time and they were both kind of rattling around in my head after the meditation. *Wait, which one is it?* I shrugged and wrote them both on the sticky note. A few days later, I was at the grocery store looking for tulips to give to a friend, and a woman across from me pulled out a couple of long stems of gladioli that I hadn't even noticed. They are a bit of an old-fashioned flower that I don't see around Seattle and aren't usually at the grocery store. Cool! Yay, Hugh. Apparently that was the sign. Then a couple of nights later, I was awakened in my sleep by his voice shouting at me, "Gladiator!" That was so funny. It was like he couldn't think of any other way to fulfill that sign.

Another time, the word "Toulouse" popped into my head. I heard it and saw it. On the sticky note it went. Weeks went by. I forgot about it. I was in downtown Seattle for a hair appointment, and while I was sitting in the salon chair, waiting for my hair color to bake, I got to thinking, *Huh, I don't think I've gotten my last sign from Hugh.* And I couldn't, for the life of me, even remember what the sign was. I was racking my brain. No luck. On the Metro bus on my way home from the appointment, I was scrolling through Instagram, and up popped a post from the Seattle Art Museum featuring their new exhibition, *Renegade Edo and Paris: Japanese Prints and Toulouse-Lautrec.* That's it! Toulouse. I remembered. The timing was perfect, considering that just a couple of hours earlier, I was wondering about the sign and what the word was.

I haven't asked Hugh for a sign in a while, so I asked him just this morning for one. The word I got made me laugh out loud. It is slightly naughty and very on point with Hugh's humor. So, the sticky is in place, and I can't wait to see how it plays out.

Suzanne's courses armed me with tools for connecting with Hugh, which I continue to use and am so grateful for. I also appreciate the gift she gave me of a greater understanding of the Universe, of Divine Love, of the infinite wisdom available to us. And—now, I'm sure this wasn't on the syllabus she wrote for the goals of her courses, but—seeing this woman who was highly structured, methodical, and disciplined become a medium made me think that my structured, methodical, disciplined self could, too.

12

SCIENCE OF THE AFTERLIFE

All the shutdowns of the pandemic created a global learning community. Distance learning had certainly existed before, but now everyone was turning their offerings online, and it became so easy to take classes on any topic, at any time, from anywhere. I was so grateful for that. I was able to go on this life-changing spiritual journey while confined to my house, in front of my computer, nursing a cup of hot tea.

A couple of months after taking Suzanne's first course—a year and a half after Hugh passed—I saw somewhere that Laura Lynne Jackson was offering an online series. It wasn't a topic I was initially interested in, but I would jump at anything from Laura Lynne. Psychic Bootcamp 101. Who knew there was such a thing?

Her course explored the four primary "clairs" of intuition that we are all said to possess beyond our five senses, and which generally go unnoticed by us in our thoughts-filled, harried, material existence:

1. **Clairvoyance:** clear *seeing* of things external of ourselves or in our minds—such as spirit—or seeing past or future events.
2. **Clairaudience:** clear *hearing* of sounds, music, thoughts, and voice of spirit.
3. **Claircognizance:** clear *knowing* of something without knowing how or why we know it.
4. **Clairsentience:** clear *feeling* of energy and the presence of spirit; also our gut instincts, first impressions of people, and ability to "read the room." This is the most common of the clairs.

These collectively make up the "sixth sense" that we've all heard about, maybe largely in movies and TV shows. In the course, there was also discussion of the seven chakras—the primary energy points in our bodies, which run down the spine, and should ideally be open and flowing to lead to good physical, mental, emotional, and spiritual health—and they are tied to the clairs as well.

Laura Lynne talked about how all objects hold energy and how touching them can help us tune into our psychic abilities. She suggested going to an antique store and experiencing what feelings and thoughts come up. She gave us students a lot of guidance on how to identify, clear, balance, and connect with energy including spirit.

What began as an attempt to connect with Hugh and learn more about mediumship started to expand into an awakening to an entirely different way of seeing the world and moving through it. I was still not working and, for the time being, wasn't looking for a new job, giving me band-width for more exploration.

By now, I had become a human sponge, eagerly soaking up all the information about this new world I'd entered that I could get a hold of. One of the most impactful learnings to me was that our thoughts are energy—as is, well, every-thing. Energy flows where our thoughts go. I'd been hear-ing a lot that intention in spiritual practices, and all of life, is essential, but hadn't made the connection that thoughts are real energy, real "things." So, have intention in your thoughts to create and manifest the things you want—don't put your energy into thinking about what you *don't* want, or your energy will flow to making those things happen. One easy example is that of debt. If your thoughts, words, wor-ries, actions are about bills and debt and getting out of debt, your energy will flow toward debt. If, on the other hand, your thoughts and words are about how to get to prosperity and financial security, your energy will move toward pros-perity and financial security.

You may be sitting there thinking, *Duh. Everyone knows the power of positive thinking.* And manifesting has become a thing since the book *The Secret* by Rhonda Byrne was published in 2006 and became an international phenom-enon. It reintroduced the Universe's law of attraction to a modern audience, which has been chronicled in literature and philosophies for centuries. But honest to goodness, I have chalked my successes up to hard work and good luck. What power there was in being opened to the idea that thoughts are energy and that we best be thoughtful about their intentions.

I am innately and ravenously curious about all things, but this was all in the category of—I don't know—woo-woo that I hadn't previously explored.

As I continued to follow Laura Lynne and subscribed to her newsletter, I saw that she was doing an online interview with Dr. Julie Beischel from the Windbridge Research Center. Dr. Beischel received her PhD in pharmacology and toxicology with a minor in microbiology and immunology from the University of Arizona. She had a traditional experience with science until her mother passed from suicide and Dr. Beischel started to ask serious questions about the afterlife. In an interview with Theresa Cheung, a researcher and internationally bestselling author on spirituality, she says, "It wasn't long before I found out that there was just too much data out there to dismiss and it needed to be investigated properly but science wasn't really addressing it." She eventually turned her rigorous, peer-reviewed scientific methodologies to investigating mediums and what they can teach us about the afterlife and the survival of consciousness. Dr. Beischel is often praised for doing the most important research on mediumship in the world.

Now, this was up my alley. I don't think I've really

explained my need to research and understand everything. I have a bachelor of science in microbiology and worked in the pharmaceutical industry for several years after college, before unexpectedly falling into marketing. That's a whole other story. But I've always had a deep interest in science and scientific methods and am known among my people to be a prolific question-asker in every aspect of my life. It is no different as I've embarked on a spiritual journey.

I watched the online interview between Laura Lynne and Dr. Beischel, and my sparse notes about it fail me. I am usually a copious notetaker, so I can only assume that I was too enrapt to take notes—because I was. Why did I choose to note this: "Dream visitations from our loved ones feel 3D, like you're in it. But dream visitations are hard for the deceased—like playing double Dutch jump rope. They have to time the brainwaves just right to get in."

One thing I remember is that Dr. Beischel used the term "the discarnate"—which is a person or being without a physical body—to scientifically identify the deceased. I got that "discarnate" certainly is an accurate scientific term, but it felt a little cold and removed from the soul or essence of a person that I was starting to understand we still are after death.

The interview led me to her book *Investigating Mediums*. Dr. Beischel opens the book by saying that one way to scientifically examine the theory that consciousness survives physical death is to investigate the phenomenon of mediumship—and that a medium is someone who "regularly, reliably, and often on-demand" experiences communication from the deceased.

She has been doing this research since 2008. Before mediums are accepted into the research program, they are screened extensively over months, using an eight-step process. If they successfully pass those eight steps, they are called a Windbridge Certified Research Medium (WCRM). Laura Lynne Jackson is one of those certified mediums, and in her book *The Light Between Us*, she describes the rigor of the testing, and her want and anticipation of getting into the program.

Dr. Beischel writes, "This program examines the abilities of mediums to report accurate and specific information about discarnates using anomalous information reception (AIR); that is, without any prior knowledge or feedback and without using deceptive or fraudulent means."

You've probably heard of double-blind studies where both the participant and the experimenter are blinded to the independent variable that is being studied—such as not knowing which participants are getting the real treatment and which the placebo. Dr. Beischel's research utilizes *quintuple*-blind investigation that accounts for fraud and biases that either the medium or sitter could have. "Sitter" is the term widely used throughout mediumship for the person who is receiving the reading, whose loved one is being connected with. The readings were all done over the phone with the medium and the sitter having no interaction.

Oh goodness, it was a puzzle to read about how all

that blinding is done. Suffice it to say that the medium was blinded to all information about the sitter and the discarnate before, during, and after the reading. The experimenter who works with the medium is also blinded to all information about the sitter and discarnate, except for the discarnate's first name. The experimenter who works with the sitter is blinded to which mediums read for which sitters and which readings were intended for which sitters. The sitters are blinded to the origin of the readings—they don't hear the reading and are given two typed-up readings—one of which is with their loved one and another that is a decoy. The sitter scores those two readings for accuracy as to how well they fit their loved one. And the experimenter who interacts with the sitter in post-scoring follow-up is blinded to whatever the heck is left.

In the reading, the medium was given only the first name of the discarnate to connect to, and the experimenter asked these questions:

1. What did the discarnate look like in his/her physical life?
2. What was the discarnate's personality?
3. What were the discarnate's hobbies or activities?
4. What was the discarnate's cause of death?
5. Does the discarnate have any comments, questions, requests, or messages for the sitter?
6. Is there anything else you can tell me about this person?

Dr. Beischel discusses in detail the hypotheses, results, probabilities, and possible explanations for the results. In the end, she found that 76 percent of the sitters picked the reading that was intended for them. So, not 100 percent, but still statistically significant when probability would be 50 percent. And that is only the beginning of the research, as the data can't prove that the mediums are communicating directly with the deceased. So, on Dr. Beischel went to other aspects of rigorous investigation.

It was a fascinating read, and the scientific-references-heavy book reassured my brain that science is investigating mediumship and—as I discovered later—all aspects of consciousness and the survival of consciousness. Science was a material tether grounding me in this journey.

But what was really the heart of the book for me was the step away from science and into simply asking the mediums about their experiences during readings:

1. What is the afterlife like?
2. How do you experience communication from the deceased?
3. What advice, suggestions, or instructions can you give to people interested in experiencing communication with their deceased loved ones on their own?
4. Why might it be that someone has not heard from their loved one when they want to?

Their answers to the afterlife question create an image of a place as bright as a million candles, filled with joy and peace, where we continue to learn and grow—and we realize that it is not actually a place at all but exists right amid our world.

I so loved the descriptions from the mediums about what it's like to connect with a spirit being. They all have very different experiences. Dr. Beischel described how, for one medium, it's like a good friend who comes knocking on her energetic door, and they sit in the living room and chat. Another described how spirits need to learn to communicate after they cross over, and some are more skilled than others—that she is like an instrument they play, and that some can play like Beethoven while others are still working on "Chopsticks."

They also said that the question they get asked in almost every reading is how people can connect with their own loved ones without needing a medium. Guilty as charged. The mediums are excited to help people learn to do this and provided wonderful specific advice and suggestions, but the general overlying thing they repeatedly said is to wholeheartedly *trust* that you can communicate with your loved ones; trust in your ability to recognize signs and notice the nudges from spirit; trust that it's not your imagination or a coincidence. They talked about how people try so hard, read all the books, meditate, go to mediums for advice (hello, Wendy Saffel, lookin' at you) when all they have to do is be open, be patient, watch for a message, and trust that it will come.

It can sound one sided, us just patiently waiting to see our loved ones' signs. One of the Windbridge mediums said that, indeed, it's up to the deceased to make contact and for the living to recognize the contact. We can study all there is to study about afterlife communication, but in the end, the ball is in their court. That felt true to my experience. Ultimately, the ball was in Hugh's court. But I also think this was why I was attracted to meditation exercises where it felt like there was more of an immediate conversation with Hugh rather than sending out a call and waiting for a response. I learned that people feel the same way about conversing with loved ones through automatic writing.

According to the mediums, a lot of people are concerned that they haven't heard from their loved ones—and sometimes the loved ones don't come through even in readings. That can be due to factors on the side of the deceased, such as their need to learn to communicate or to grow or work through things like guilt before they are ready to come through—or it can be due to factors on the side of the living person, such as grief, skepticism, trying too hard, or an inability to recognize subtle forms of communication.

I look back at this heavily marked-up, dog-eared, tabbed book, and it's evident to me that I was being convinced by both the scientific methodology and by the experiences of the mediums.

Another essential name to bring into this topic of

science-based research is that of Gary E. Schwartz, PhD, who directs the Laboratory for Advances in Consciousness and Health (lach.org). In 2024, Dr. Schwartz retired from his professorship in psychology, medicine, neurology, psychiatry, and surgery at the University of Arizona. After receiving his doctorate from Harvard University in psychophysiology, he worked there as an assistant professor. He then served as a professor of psychology and psychiatry at Yale University, directed the Yale Psychophysiology Center, and codirected the Yale Behavioral Medicine Clinic. Dr. Schwartz has published more than five hundred scientific papers, including six in the journal *Science*, and is a fellow in multiple scientific associations. He served as the founding president of the Academy for the Advancement of Postmaterial Sciences. Seven of his books—*The Living Energy Universe, The Afterlife Experiments, The Energy Healing Experiments, The Truth about Medium, The Sacred Promise, An Atheist in Heaven,* and *Extraordinary Claims Require Extraordinary Evidence*—are related to his scientific investigations and findings addressing the survival-of-consciousness hypothesis. Impressive credentials—the kind I craved as I dove into the science of all this, seeking evidence-based proof of mediumship and afterlife studies.

Dr. Schwartz has risked his academic reputation to prove or disprove the existence of an afterlife. I have had the blessing of seeing him present in person. A humble, kind, and great human, he talks passionately about his love of photons, which can be both a particle and a wave. He uses relatable examples to show how photons have captured all information about the universe that ever was. The photons that were present during the Big Bang billions of years ago are still present and vibrating in our rooms today. The information therein lasts as long as the light lasts. And so it is with our being. Or with animals, or even art, cars, or houses—the photons of anything with form never die.

Dr. Schwartz says, "Science is actually inadvertently and often unknowingly providing some of the best theoretical and empirical evidence for a greater reality, which deserves awe, respect, and love." He says that quantum physics— along with documented near-death experiences, afterlife communication, children who remember past lives, and the emergence of technology that can interact with spirit— show beyond a reasonable doubt the survival of consciousness. Dr. Schwartz has also worked with some of the most prominent American mediums and validated their abilities with his rigorous scientific methods. This research was showcased with gripping results in his book *The Afterlife Experiments: Breakthrough Scientific Evidence of Life After Death*. He is looking at this topic from all angles.

What I summarize here is science lite. So, so, so lite. I don't profess for a second to having one iota of knowledge about the depth of any of it. This was a shallow skimming of the surface. The reason it was important to me to dip my toes in these waters, though, is that I am reticent to buy into anything hook, line, and sinker. As I embarked on an unseeable spiritual path, my confidence was bolstered to know that really, really brilliant people with well-defined scientific methodologies are proving that this is true. If this is important to you, too, I urge you to do your own homework and do what it takes to convince yourself. But, all this does beg the question: Why is there now so much research being conducted?

When I burrowed into further research, I came upon social historian Julia Assante, PhD, who has her doctorate from Columbia University and is also a medium. In her book *The Last Frontier: Exploring the Afterlife and Transforming Our Fear of Death*, she says, "In the past few decades, we have witnessed an explosion of information about death and the afterlife, generated by an ever-growing number of psychologists and psychiatrists, physicians, hospice nurses and bereavement counselors, near-death experiencers, researchers in parapsychology, and of course, mediums, who are working toward a better understanding of the world to come." She marvels at how every one of us will enter the last frontier of death and what comes next, yet our culture has made little attempt to understand and chart this. Instead, we pour billions into exploring outer space—and how many of us will go there?

It's time for this research in an era where there is a revolution of interest in the topic. There certainly was for me. Having a loved one pass activates people in different ways. This research and the spiritual journey were calling to me, and I don't know why it would for me more than for someone else in the same situation, but I began to feel that it was going to be more and more defining of my life.

13

A GLIMPSE INTO
THE DEVELOPMENT
OF MEDIUMS

It was now eighteen months since Hugh had passed, and I was practicing ways to communicate with him almost daily. All the while, my need to learn more about the phenomenon of mediumship was growing stronger and stronger. After doing all the research I could on the science of mediumship and deciding this was all legit, I made a decision that surprised me and dramatically altered the course of my life. I—the skeptic—would study to become a medium.

I never expected to go on this life-changing spiritual journey after the death of my son. And I really, really, *really* never expected to become interested in studying mediumship and developing as a medium myself. But more than anything else—more than all the research, all the reading,

all the summits and workshops, all the signs, all the *beliefs*—
studying and experiencing mediumship has brought me full
circle to *knowing* with certainty that there is life after death,
that we absolutely can communicate and continue relationships with our loved ones in spirit, and that it brings tremendous healing and peace.

I think it might be interesting for you to get a look into
what it's like to develop as a medium, how it works, what it
feels like, and if it can be considered normal to talk to dead
people. Even if you have absolutely no interest in studying
mediumship yourself, it certainly is fascinating at the very
least. And to that, I would also add miraculous and sacred.

Where to begin explaining the course of my studies and
ongoing development as a medium? There have been three
predominant concepts I've picked up from different teachers that have been most impactful in my understanding of
mediumship: It uses the *language of energy*, and *the art of
feeling*, to *communicate soul to soul* with people who are no
longer in their bodies.

Let's start with energy. As previously noted, we are all
made up of energy. Everything is energy. The steel beams
holding up your office building are energy. That mountain
you're going to hike around this weekend is energy. Our
thoughts and feelings are energy. And the law of conservation of energy states that energy can neither be created nor
destroyed—only converted from one form of energy to another. All this was easy for me to get behind because of the
science, those quantum mechanics, and the multiple Nobel

Prize–winning physicists who have proven this time and time again.

When a person passes away, their energy is still here.

On the National Public Radio (NPR) program *All Things Considered*, commentator Aaron Freeman gives advice for planning your funeral, beautifully illustrated as:

"You want a physicist to speak at your funeral. You want the physicist to talk to your grieving family about the conservation of energy, so they will understand that your energy has not died. You want the physicist to remind your sobbing mother about the first law of thermodynamics; that no energy gets created in the universe, and none is destroyed. You want your mother to know that all your energy, every vibration, every Btu of heat, every wave of every particle that was her beloved child remains with her in this world. You want the physicist to tell your weeping father that amid energies of the cosmos, you gave as good as you got.

"And at one point you'd hope that the physicist would step down from the pulpit and walk to your brokenhearted spouse there in the pew and tell him that all the photons that ever bounced off your face, all the particles whose paths were interrupted by your smile, by the touch of your hair, hundreds of trillions of particles, have raced off like children, their ways forever changed by you. And as your widow rocks in the arms of a loving family, may the physicist let her know that all the photons that bounced from you were gathered in the particle detectors that are her eyes,

that those photons created within her constellations of elec-
tromagnetically charged neurons whose energy will go on
forever.

"And the physicist will remind the congregation of how
much of all our energy is given off as heat. There may be a
few fanning themselves with their programs as he says it.
And he will tell them that the warmth that flowed through
you in life is still here, still part of all that we are, even as we
who mourn continue the heat of our own lives.

"And you'll want the physicist to explain to those who
loved you that they need not have faith; indeed, they should
not have faith. Let them know that they can measure, that
scientists have measured precisely the conservation of energy and found it accurate, verifiable and consistent across
space and time. You can hope your family will examine the
evidence and satisfy themselves that the science is sound
and that they'll be comforted to know your energy's still
around. According to the law of the conservation of energy,
not a bit of you is gone; you're just less orderly. Amen."

THE LANGUAGE OF ENERGY

So, how can mediums communicate with the consciousness of our loved one whose energy is not orderly, who has
no vocal cords to speak, no eyes to see, or ears to hear? They
converse through the language of energy. After having that
early mediumship reading with Marie Manuchehri that

rocked my world when Hugh came through so clearly and profoundly, and after traveling a long and winding road of spiritual discovery afterward and becoming interested in mediumship, three years after Hugh passed, I did a three-month mentorship with Marie and twenty other students. She teaches that every one of us is fluent in the language of energy, as we have lived many in-between lifetimes on the Other Side and that has always been our first language. Every person of every culture, of every country, of every language, of every century speaks that same language on the Other Side. We have just forgotten it on this human journey.

So, every one of us has access to this realm, this possibility. But just as with gifted athletes, or gifted artists, gifted teachers, gifted anything, some people are more naturally inclined to this than others and have had experiences with spirit their entire lives. I'm not one of those people. It can be learned. Whether you're wanting to become a medium, or just develop your abilities in order to connect with your own loved ones, I tell you that if I can do it, you can do it. It is a skill, which can be acquired.

SOUL-TO-SOUL COMMUNICATION

In the mediumship courses I've taken from Suzanne Giesemann, she calls mediumship "soul-to-soul communication." The soul is often defined in many religious traditions as the spiritual nature of a person, which includes a person's identity, personality, and memories—a nonmaterial aspect of a living being that is believed to be able to survive physical death. That sounds a lot to me like how the scientific and philosophical traditions define consciousness, maybe minus the spiritual aspect. Many say that the soul and consciousness are the same thing. Others say that they are very different. I have pondered that in the same way I have pondered consciousness versus the mind. Or the mind versus the brain. I have arrived at thinking that it just doesn't matter what I or anyone else calls it. I think it's really the essence of the person you're communicating with, all those things taken together that makes them like no one else in all of time and creation. In connecting with spirits beyond the veil, it's really one's soul that is connecting with the soul or essence of the person who has passed through the language of energy.

As I take you on the journey of development as a medium, we will talk much about the other predominant concept of mediumship that I have gathered from my learning, which is that it's the art of feeling. We will explore that more deeply.

THE ART OF FEELING: ENERGETIC AWARENESS

I must first declare that I'm not an expert at anything. Nothing other than my own lived experience. There might be mediums or some of my teachers that read this book and think I've gotten some things wrong. That said, this is what mediumship is for *me*.

There are so many terrific mediumship teachers and coaches out there. There's a feeling of generosity in the community because there just aren't enough well-developed, accurate, ethical, evidence-based mediums. The more great mediums there are, the more it serves humanity. There isn't a feeling of competition, and most mediums will tell you that you don't actually need one in order to communicate with your loved ones. I've even heard some of the greats say they would be happy to go out of business if it meant that everyone could do it on their own. It is always, always about serving the highest good for all. I see mediumship as a birthright since I now know that we all can speak that language of energy with people in spirit.

Even though I see it as a birthright, it hasn't made learning to be a medium easy. It has been a thousand times harder than I expected it to be. I've been lucky to have great teachers, and boy, do they have their work cut out for them.

The one that really took me from zero to something was Michael Mayo. I was introduced to him through a course of his I took at the Shift Network—Evidence-Based Mediumship to Confidently Connect with Loved Ones & the Spirit World. While some mediums have highly structured systems—which I initially thought would be perfect for me, but later felt were too rigid—Michael's methods are very organic and simple. I continued to study with him at his Oakbridge Institute—a teaching community based in

California but fully online, dedicated to raising the standard of excellence in mediumship and psychic awareness.

His is an interesting story, as each medium's is. When he was eighteen, a friend invited him to a large group mediumship reading, and he thought, *Huh? What? OK,* and went. In an auditorium filled with people, the medium zeroed in on Michael, walked up to him, and said, "You're a medium, you need to start developing, and one day, you'll be doing what I'm doing." Michael was bewildered. He had had no exposure to mediumship and didn't even really know what it was. It piqued his interest, though, and afterward he found a practice group to try out. When it was his turn to do a reading, he knocked it out of the park and brought through much accurate information from those in spirit without any knowledge of how to do that, with no training. Everyone was dazzled and couldn't believe it was his first time. When Michael returned the following week, he got nothing. Then more nothing. Then continued nothing for a long, long time. It's as if spirit wanted to show him that he had a gift, then made him work for it. It's a good thing, because the reason Michael is such a gifted teacher is that he had to work so hard to figure it out. I asked another medium if she would be interested in teaching, and she said that she would have absolutely no idea how to teach mediumship since the ability had just always been turned on for her. Michael was in development with some of the best mediums in the world for five years before he started working with the public.

I took Michael's Foundations I, II, and III courses, which

took up most of the second year after Hugh passed. One of the first things he said in the first class holds completely true for me still, years after taking that initial course. "Our thinking mind is the only thing getting in the way of making a connection with spirit."

When I heard that, I thought, *Uh oh.* I have meditated for years and have been at complete odds with my thinking, sometimes regarding it as a foe. In trying to quiet or observe the mind, the term "monkey mind" is used a lot in the meditation world and is a good analogy for the busy, screeching, distracted mind swinging from branch to branch to branch. Now that I have a hummingbird feeder outside my kitchen window, I think, *Nah, I've got hummingbird mind*—their tiny hearts pounding at 1,200 beats per minute, their wings a blur, hovering, flitting off in any direction at any second and fighting off any other hummers, completely unwilling to cohabitate at a feeder. That's my mind. How is this going to work?

Our minds make things up. Lots and lots and lots of things. All the time. In fact, who we are is largely the *story* of who we are that our minds tell ourselves. And our realities are largely made up of our perceptions and beliefs. So it is in the early stages of mediumship development. Once we learn to actually make a link with spirit, which we'll get to later, we are uncomfortable with the stillness, and our minds actively go after information rather than letting it come to us. And when we actually do get some information, our minds want to fill in gaps that often aren't accurate. The

other thing our minds can do is tell ourselves that we're absolute crap at this. Or that we're stupid or barking up the
wrong tree in wanting to do this.

Michael teaches that there are three things that create
tension and get in the way in mediumship:

1. **Desire** for a specific outcome, or to make a
   connection.
2. **Distraction** of our thoughts, beliefs, and biases.
3. **Expectation** that a reading is supposed to go
   a certain way. At that point, we're pursuing,
   rather than being neutral.

All created by the mind.

It ends up that I am pretty clairvoyant (clear seeing) and
see a lot of images. Sometimes it's 100 percent accurate as
I relay it to the sitter, and sometimes it's not at all. Michael
teaches that you can't always trust what you see, since our
minds can make it up. Man, our minds are a powerful, powerful force. So, if it gets in the way in mediumship, what do
you do?

This is where the art of *feeling* comes in.

Clairsentience (clear feeling) is truly the foundation of
mediumship. It can't be made up in our minds like images
and thoughts can. I think there are two kinds of feeling in
mediumship: physical sensations and emotional impressions.

For the first, there is a special meditation called Sitting

in the Power, which is considered essential by many mediums. I've heard time and again that Sitting in the Power often and long is more beneficial to mediumship than practice readings are. The more you do it, the more you progress. This exercise helps you build your personal power, raise your vibration, and expand your energetic awareness so you can feel when spirit moves into your field. It is different from the meditation I mentioned learning from Suzanne earlier in that the intention here is not to communicate with anyone in spirit, but to broaden your sensitivities to understand your own energy and to pick up energy coming from another source, any spirit person who might be coming in.

I think every meditation ever starts with deep breaths to calm your nervous system and still the body. From here, there are many interpretations of Sitting in the Power. I'll tell you what works best for me, which is an amalgamation of many. You can find numerous Sitting in the Power exercises online.

- Set an intention that this practice be sacred and for the highest good of all.
- Take three deep breaths. Breathe in love and exhale fear. Breathe in peace and exhale stress. Breathe in trust and exhale doubt.
- Consider your feet, and imagine them upon Mother Earth, and give thanks for her sustaining you in this life and for keeping you grounded during the work of mediumship.

- Imagine a bright white light in the center of your body, wherever that is to you. For me, it's in my solar plexus, but it might be your abdomen or your heart space. This is your life-force energy, the love and light of your soul. And as you breathe, the light grows bigger and brighter until it fills the whole of your body, and your every vein and cell is filled with the love and the light of your soul.

- Imagine your light, your energy, moving out through your skin. In front of and behind you. Above and below you. To the left and the right of you.

- And with each breath, your energy expands until it fills the room.

- And here you sit for a time to get familiar with what *your* energy feels like. That alone is interesting. For me, it just feels neutral. I don't feel much because I think I'm used to my own energy.

- When you feel ready, invite your spirit guides and helpers into your energy field to develop you as you need to be developed today. Ask that this be their time to do what is needed for you today. And thank them.

- Sit with no expectations. No agenda. Only neutral awareness. Notice any changes in the atmosphere around you.

- For weeks, I didn't notice much as spirit came in. Then I started to feel things. I could feel something move into my field. Tickles. Tingles. Buzzing. Pressure. Cold. Heat. A puff of air. It's important to not engage with what you're feeling, but to just notice, accept, and let it go. Notice, accept, let it go.
- Of course, your mind is really busy, but try to let thoughts float away like clouds, and center on your breathing again. Notice, accept, let it go.
- These steps should be done slowly, not rushed. I can typically do this for fifteen minutes. Thirty would be better. An hour would be amazing. Teacher Michael has always said that doing this at least four times a week is necessary.
- Upon closing your meditation, thank your guides and helpers for working with you today.

This is really a shorthand. Some versions have you do a feet-to-head relaxation of all body parts before starting. Some versions have you move your energy into that of the Divine's so that your energies are blended before inviting your guides and helpers in. Or to consciously raise your vibration and energy to match that of spirit, which some people consider to be the "shift" needed in order to connect. And some have different intentions altogether. I incorporate bits of all these at times, but this is the one I use most, which has helped me become sensitive to spirit. Even experienced mediums Sit in the Power regularly. Once in a regular practice of energetic awareness, a medium can quickly do an attunement before a reading, which shifts them from a thinking mind to awareness.

Energetic awareness is essential in a reading.

I can now easily tell when spirit has arrived. I can tell if it's male or female. I can discern forceful or frenetic energy from calm or reserved energy. Spirit can evoke feelings in my body that relate to physical ailments or injuries they had, or their cause of death.

And my mind isn't making any of this up.

Equally important is the emotional impressions a medium gets from all the varied information coming in, also not of the mind. We'll tackle that next.

THE ART OF FEELING:
EMOTIONAL IMPRESSIONS

This is all just the tip of the iceberg of my developing as a medium. The other day, I got a beautiful Windows Spotlight image that came up on my computer screen showing a side view of an iceberg in what you could just tell was cold, cold blue Arctic waters. You could see the chunk of ice above the water and the colossal, no-end-in-sight amount of ice below the waterline. That so perfectly illustrated for me the infinite depth of what a medium must develop before they would ever put someone's tender, grieving heart in their hands.

Another important thing I learned about becoming a medium was that spirit doesn't communicate in the I-feel-crappy channel. So says highly regarded medium, medical intuitive, and author Julie Ryan in a video teaching people how to prepare themselves to communicate with their loved ones. This is a good explanation for one of the reasons why we often don't feel the presence of, or recognize the signs from, our loved ones when we're deep in grief. Just when we want and need our loved one most, we're smothered in a gray, hazy, low-energy fog of pain.

Such is also the case when trying to make a mediumistic connection with someone else's loved one in spirit. For me, the low-energy I-feel-crappy channel is a self-imposed state of self-doubt and fear. Fear of not making a connection. Fear of getting the information all wrong. Fear of my mind making things up. Fear of getting the "no" from my practice partner when I narrate what I'm receiving. Fear of not doing as well as my practice partner. This is a 100 percent common experience for mediums in the early stages of development, and one of the reasons why development takes so long until a person can move to a feeling of confidence and trust in themself and spirit. Then communication really starts flowing.

As mentioned earlier, the three things that create tension and get in the way of mediumship—desire, distraction, and expectation—are the everything, and the root of self-doubt. Michael teaches people to come into a reading with absolutely no expectation of the outcome. What does it really matter as a student if you do a practice reading and get nothing? What does it matter if your last reading was magnificent and in this one you struggle? And you actually learn a lot from a "no" that your partner gives you when what you're saying doesn't ring true. It teaches you that the information came from your mind, or that you tried to interpret it rather than just narrating what you're getting. You learn how that feels different from true, inspired spirit communication. As with all things in life, the struggle teaches us.

Initially, when I was not working and was able to fully devote myself to my development, I went into each practice reading with great determination and expectation. About eighteen months into my studies, I went back to work, and my schedule became more hectic. It turned out that my inability to overprepare actually proved to be a good thing. Now, I Sit in the Power as much as I can—at least four times a week—and I just show up to practice. I am always so grateful to have the opportunity to practice with wonderful, supportive, nonjudgmental people. Over time, my trust kept growing and growing that spirit is always there and never wrong, and will help me.

In healing practices like mediumship and Reiki—which I also started studying during this journey, eventually culminating in me receiving my Reiki III Master certificate—the practitioner asks the Universe for help in doing what is in the highest good for the person they are working with, and in the highest good for all. That is paramount in the ethics of healing, as is the same Hippocratic oath that doctors take: First, do no harm. Nowadays, my prayer and intention going into a reading is always that I be used in a way that is in the highest good for the other person.

This is the way Michael sets students up to start a reading. After a short preparation of focusing on the breath, feeling the Divine spark within filling your body, imagining your energy growing to fill the room, and attuning to the energy of your own being, there is an invocation to spirit in our mind:

Spirit, please help me get out of the way.

Help me follow your lead.

I can't do this without you.

To that, I add:

Let your thoughts become my thoughts. Your voice, my voice.

And after the invocation, surrender. The more you let go, the more things will happen. The more a person has Sat in the Power and is attuned to their own energy field and to spirit, the more they can feel when someone steps in. I typically feel a pressure or tightening in my solar plexus—which is a compilation of nerves located near your diaphragm, and the location of one of the chakras. It's been said that this is the center of clairsentience (clear feeling), so it makes sense that this is where I feel spirit step in. Sometimes, information starts coming in so quickly that I don't even get to the point of physically sensing spirit.

For example, I was once paired in a breakout room with a woman named Amanda, whom I had never worked with before. She likes the practice of "going direct" and asking your partner who they want to communicate with. More often, a medium simply opens to who wants and needs to come through and trusts that the spirits who will be most meaningful to the client will be there. Since Amanda asked me who I wanted to hear from, I did the same when it was time to read her. It actually simplifies things since you're not trying to determine gender or the relationship the spirit has to the person.

She wanted to hear from her grandmother Verlene. For some reason, over Zoom, I thought I heard Amanda say Erlene, which I repeated back to her. And she corrected me to what I then thought was Berlene, and corrected me again to Verlene with a *V.* Then, I immediately heard an uproarious laugh and saw a grandmotherly figure standing in an apron, saying, "Well, this will be fun." She had a huge smile, and I saw sparkles in her eyes.

What transpired was a good example of the art of *feeling*, which Michael always taught us to lean into when we *see* something in a reading, since seeing can't always be trusted. What are the emotional impressions from the information coming in? What did that image make me *feel*? From the image I saw and the voice I heard, I felt that this was a fun woman of good cheer, high energy, not shy.

"Yes," said Amanda as I narrated that. Without seeing anything specific, I got a *feeling*, or maybe it was a *knowing*, that Amanda and her grandmother had lived close to each other and spent a lot of time together, were part of each other's lives on a daily basis. (This was different from my own experience of living states away from my two grandmothers.)

"Yes," said Amanda. I saw many images of her and her grandmother, always with their heads together, bending over something. Working in the garden. Doing some kind of needlework. I got the *feeling* that her grandmother was teaching her many things, not just that they were enjoying those things together.

"Absolutely." And I only ever saw Amanda and her grandmother in all these visions. No parents. No other siblings or grandkids. I had a strong *feeling* that this meant something. I mentioned this to Amanda, and I also said, "She is very focused on you, and I feel that she was very present and made you feel like you were the most important person in her life."

"Bingo. I *was* the most important person in her life."

I then internally asked Amanda to grow up in my visions and saw her later caring for her grandmother. I narrated that and said, "I feel that your grandmother wasn't the same person she was earlier in your life."

"That's correct." I started to feel like I was going to cry, and love just welled up in my body. So much love and emotion. I knew how much her grandmother loved her and how happy she was to still be part of Amanda's life. How proud she was of Amanda and this work she was doing. And I also knew that she was whole, happy, and her usual energetic self on the Other Side.

Amanda and I had agreed to do just short readings—seven minutes. I like that because you don't have as much time to get into your head as in a longer reading. So, I ended it with that message of profound love and pride from her grandmother. I was eager to hear about Verlene. Amanda relayed the story of her own mother telling Verlene that if she couldn't take Amanda, Amanda would have to go to a foster home due to things going on with Amanda's mother. So, her grandmother raised her. She taught Amanda everything: gardening, canning, quilt-making, life-living, and they were inseparable. Her grandmother actually told all the other grandkids that Amanda was her favorite. And Amanda was, indeed, involved in her grandmother's care after she had an amputation and cognitive decline—definitely not the woman she had been. Amanda thought there were many things that came through in the short reading that were right on, and she thanked me so much for bringing her beloved grandmother through.

There are plenty of other readings where things are harder to figure out. It may be that I'm having an off day. Or the person in spirit may be reserved and not very talkative, which can happen because we maintain our same personality when we cross over. Sometimes, I try different things to get information. I mentioned before how influential Laura Lynne Jackson's books were for me. I particularly liked *The Light Between Us*, in which she shares her journey to understanding and using her gifts for good.

Just a few months ago, I had a spiritual assessment four

years after Hugh passed, with a gifted medium who said, "Have you read Laura Lynne Jackson's books? I've never actually asked anyone that before. I haven't read them myself."

"Yes, I have read them!" I say.

She replied, "I'm being told that you should revisit the books and pay attention to the grid."

I knew exactly what she was talking about. Laura Lynne, a schoolteacher, imagines a whiteboard where she asks spirit to come into different sections on her whiteboard that tell her certain things. I decided to give that a try because one of the hardest things for me is determining what the relationship of the spirit is to the sitter. I wrote out a grid where I had sections, like a tic-tac-toe board, broken into categories: Parent, Grandparent, Aunt/Uncle, Partner, Child, Sibling/Cousin, Friend/Colleague. It sounds complicated, but I got it down. When I struggle with the relationship, I will imagine that grid and ask spirit to step into the right section for their relationship. I will see a point of light in that section, and it has been correct as I narrate the relationship to the sitter.

I have so many stories, and I've done so many readings that have been truly rewarding, and meaningful to my practice partners—evidence that their loved one is indeed right here, right now. I don't know what I will ever do with this or if I will be a professional medium. I find over and over that what this journey of research has done for me is prove to myself that life after death, and the possibility of communicating with our loved ones in spirit, is so very real. I'm not just a bereaved mother desperately wanting to believe it's true. And the most important part of it all for me is that it has brought me to be able to communicate better with my son.

14

TALES FROM PRACTICE CIRCLES

GRAMMY

One of the completely unexpected and wonderful benefits of developing as a medium is that you get to have a lot of mini readings done on you, and hear from your loved ones often. In addition to the practice with fellow students in classes, it is strongly encouraged that you join practice circles with other developing mediums from anywhere, online, which gives you endless new material—people you've never worked with before, and their loved ones in spirit. It is excellent practice. It also teaches you to be a really good sitter when you have a lot of readings done on you. Don't tell your practice partners anything about yourself or your loved ones. Answer their questions with yes, no, or I don't know, without going into explanations or giving too much information. Try to have your energy be open and support-ive. Readings go so much better that way. And be patient if the information coming through doesn't make complete sense at first, because it unfolds. After your partner has practiced on you, you give them feedback about how things hit, and that's the opportunity to tell them about the loved one that came through and how it relates to what your part-ner was communicating. You always do that with the ut-most kindness toward each other.

I've come to realize how much our loved ones in spirit are game to help out in this process. I feel that there is a real generosity among them. They're not here just for us, to give healing by coming through, but also for our practice part-ner, to give them spirit to practice on.

Just as Grammy has come through a lot in the profes-sional readings I've had since Hugh passed, she also does in my practice readings. In a few, she's been described as loving the outdoors, which I didn't remember about her. But not long ago, I revisited the binder of materials she put to-gether for all the members of our family before she passed, which has her life story as well as a ton of incredible ge-nealogy research she did on the family—old school, before all the DNA ancestry tests now. Her story is filled with a deep love of the ranch where her family lived, on a rock ledge above the Apishapa River in Colorado, and how she and her sister loved to watch the river when it was in flood, waiting for the first muddy stuff to come around the bend of the river. The pollywogs she would collect after the flood left dry creek beds, and watching the pollywogs turn into frogs. The infamous story of Grammy and her sister riding horseback naked. And how whenever she visited her grandparents in town, she would run first to the pink rose bush with tight buds and inhale the fragrance that she had never smelled anywhere else. Ah yes, she did so love the outdoors, and I didn't even remember that about her. She was also a spectacular writer, of her story and in the bundle of letters she and I wrote to each other when I was in college, which I saved and cherish.

When she comes through, it is always with words of encouragement:

- "Hey, kid, let's talk!"
- "I am here. I am with you."
- "You're on the right path."
- "Just keep going, keep trying. It'll happen."
- "You will write about this."

Sometimes, Hugh makes an appearance after her in these practice readings, just as he did in the early professional readings. I've often reflected on that and wondered why Grammy comes through first, why they're joined at the hip.

I recently took myself on a writing retreat and, while doing research, came across a video of medium Julie Ryan, who had that great quote about spirit not communicating in the "I-feel-crappy channel." She said that in her thousands of readings, she has seen that when we pass, the crossing and welcome to the Other Side is run by our mother. If our mother is still living, then by our mother's mother. And in Hugh's case, if the mother's mother is still living, then by the mother's mother's mother—always on the maternal side. If that's the case, Grammy was running the show—she would have hosted the descendants and angels when Hugh passed, and wrapped him in warm, tender, light-filled love so he was not afraid or alone. And in the first readings I had with mediums, I'm sure Grammy was showing Hugh how to do it, and was supporting him.

When Julie was asked about how it works when a person is adopted, she said that it's all about the mother who raised the person. The adoptive mother, or her mother—that maternal line—are always running the show. If the birth-mother has crossed, her spirit is definitely there, too, but it's the adoptive mother's side that is creating the loving embrace.

Now, when I reflect on this photograph of Hugh with Grammy when he was ten months old, I know they had a soul connection from the beginning, something neither of them could have known in the beautiful moment.

Ten-month-old Hugh and Grammy at her ninetieth birthday party.

UNCLE GARRY

My Uncle Garry. Easily one of the most unforgettable people I've ever known. Ever. Mischievous.

It was hard to tell when he was pulling your leg and when he was tellin' it straight, but if he got cross with you, you'd know it for sure. You'd get the hairy eyeball fast. But he was also a huge teddy bear of a man and a wonderful father and husband and uncle. He married my dad's sister and was a schoolteacher as well as a farmer. My family's trips to see our Colorado clan every other year always included a trip to see my aunt, uncle, and cousins on their farm. It was so amazing being there—a life nothing like mine. Hard physical work, long hot days, so much food, dogs, and fun.

Uncle Garry died in 2006. We didn't see each other often and weren't really close because of the infrequent gatherings, but I looked up to him and thought he was a really cool uncle.

Boy, was I surprised when he came through in a reading with a professional medium and again in a practice circle a week and a half later. The medium described him as an older balding male wearing a collared button-up Western shirt and boots. Machismo, but with a twinkle in his eyes. She enjoyed his energy and gave me other information that easily identified him. He ultimately left me with three messages:

- "You are capable of more."
- "You have everything you need."
- "It's a team effort."

It was after this reading that I decided I need to come to sessions with a list of my people in spirit and everything that makes them *them*, because when information comes through, I could be racking my brain to think of who it could be since I currently have thirteen loved ones in spirit. I'm accustomed to hearing from Grammy and Hugh, so when this older male came through, I was mentally running through the list of Grampy, Grandpa, my father-in-law, Uncle Larry, Uncle Garry. . . .

Uncle Garry! How delightful to hear from him! What a surprise. I loved knowing that he is part of my Team of Light. When the medium connected with Hugh later in the reading, she said he was definitely with the uncle. They have subsequently come through together in other readings.

Then, less than two weeks later, my practice partner invited my loved ones forward and said that she had an older man behind her. He felt very much like an old Western cowboy, with boots, chewing tobacco, and was a little rough. She kept getting the feeling of "going west" and that he was a man of faith because there was a purple color around him, which he was. At one point, after my partner communicated about him, she asked him to step out of her energy field so she could try and connect with other spirits, and he wouldn't leave. He tapped her on the right shoulder and said, "Hey, little missy."

Uncle Garry! *This is so interesting. Why has he come forward twice in such a short period of time?* I reflected on this for quite a while:

- It sure is a team effort—just like he said. I wouldn't have previously thought that he and I are very connected, but this just shows that our souls are forever connected with our loved ones and we have a team of people in spirit loving us and supporting us. I actually got teary thinking about how he was coming forward to give me encouragement.

- I had this realization that in all the practice readings, it would put a burden on Grammy and Hugh to have to come through every week and give my partners practice. So more of my Team of Light needs to step in. Uncle Garry is a perfect person to come through because he is just so describable. Such a distinctive look and personality.

Thank you, Uncle Garry. I really appreciate you letting me know that you're with me. I learned a lot by you coming through. I wonder which of my other spirit people I'll get to hear from. I can't wait.

GRAMPY

Yesterday, my practice partner Natalie hit it out of the park. I know it was such a confidence builder for her. I have come to get excited about wondering which of my loved ones will come through in these readings. I have heard from Hugh and Grammy often. And now Uncle Garry has come through, which is super fun. And yesterday . . .

"I sense an older male. He seems shaky and feeble at the end of his life," says Natalie.

"I have several older males in spirit," I respond. "I can't wait to know who this is."

"He is not a loudmouth. And he laughs when I say that. He is a nice, sweet person. I'm getting a name, Bill."

OMG, Grampy, Bill! He absolutely was not a loudmouth and would have, indeed, laughed when she said that. In fact, he rarely spoke. He was a man of the fewest words possible. I remember a family gathering when visiting Grammy and Grampy—Grampy said something and my toddler nephew gasped, wide-eyed, and said, "Grampy can talk!" He had already taken in the fact that dear, thoughtful Grampy rarely spoke. In the reading, Grampy said that he's been wanting to be in touch and was so happy to be here with me. Told me not to worry so much or try so hard. Wanted me to know that it's all really peace and love where he is. Natalie said his energy felt very gentle and that she really felt like he was helping her. Of course Grampy would help her. He helped everybody and anybody here on earth. In his decades-long career as a State Farm insurance agent, people would show up at his door, day and night, needing help with their insurance stuff, and Grampy was *always* there for them. Natalie even said she saw a building at his house where people came and went. She couldn't quite figure out what that was, but it was actually very accurate because he had converted their detached garage into his home office, and people did come and go daily. He would definitely be helping Natalie, too, grow in her mediumship, as well as being there to support and encourage me—and give me words of wisdom.

Through Natalie, he also said that he knew how much I love my walks in the forest. That kind of blew my mind because we live across the street from a forest, and I walk there every chance I can and absolutely treasure time among the ferns and towering cedar, hemlock, and maple trees; the cacophony of birds; the nested barred owls and the rabbits; the occasional coyote. It is a place of awe and spirituality for me. Grammy and Grampy had never visited us at this house or known about the importance of this forest for me. Now, whenever I walk there, I know Grampy is with me.

I felt really emotional hearing from him. It touched me deeply. Grampy passed in 1996—a long, long time ago—and it's so comforting to me to realize that our loved ones across the veil will be there for us *always*.

GRANDMA

The steering wheel sealed the deal.

After the reading where Uncle Garry came through and I thought I should have a list of my loved ones for future readings, in my project-manager spreadsheet-loving way, I put my people all on paper along with their facts, characteristics, essences, key stories. That way, when they come through, I can be a good sitter and know who it is right away. It was good, and fun, and touching to reflect on each of them and make notes about who they were. I mean, *are*.

After doing my spreadsheet yesterday morning, I had a practice circle in the afternoon. My partner Terrence blew it out of the water, as he always did when we were paired, with how much information immediately started flowing from him, and it was very specific. He clearly already is a medium. (I know, Michael Mayo says we are *all* mediums. . . .) Terrence said, "I've got an older woman coming through, petite, slight, but with strength and strong opinions underneath. She was a widow, and really came into herself as a widow." This is Grandma or my mother-in-law. Check.

I told Terrence that I had two people who fit the bill, and I was eager to find out who this was. He asked her for more specific information about herself. "Grandmotherly, on your father's side. Spent time together when you were young, cooked together." And then he said, "She could barely see

over the steering wheel of her car. She had to sit on a book."
OMG and hallelujah. At four foot eleven, Grandma was the
tiniest person ever and, indeed, had to sit on a dictionary to
see over the steering wheel of her car. We always wondered
how her feet could even touch the gas and brake pedals.

Isn't that level of specificity miraculous? Doesn't it just
blow your mind that our loved ones in spirit can show us
evidence that they are here, now? Grandma further told
Terrence that I had made an effort to visit her often and
that I introduced her to my boyfriend or fiancé. Yes, my now
husband and I traveled to see her in Colorado, and I have
pictures of us enjoying looking at photo albums with her.
Her message to me was that I had advocated for her in later
years, and she really appreciated that. I'm really touched
that I did something that was important to her.

In practice readings, I have also heard several times
from my beautiful friend Linda, who passed from cancer.
She and I had many wonderful experiences together, including traveling to Peru for a yoga retreat and healing journey
many years ago, details of which come through in readings.
I've also heard from my cousin Kerry and from the children
of some of my friends who are on the same grief journey I'm
on now. I love conveying to them when I've heard from their
kids, with messages.

In this writing process, I've asked myself why I think it's
important to include these practice readings. It really is because with my grandparents and uncle especially, they all
passed a long, long time ago. These readings showed me that

our loved ones are always with us in a very real way, supporting us, even decades later. So, if ever you are anxious to know if your child, your spouse, your parents, your best friend will still be there with you and for you in the many years to come—the answer is yes.

15

THE GIVE BACK

Around the time I was finishing up my mediumship course-work with Michael Mayo, I experienced the best day I'd had since Hugh passed two and a half years earlier. This day, one of my favorite days ever, started eleven months after Hugh passed, over coffee with an acquaintance—a wonderful, generous, philanthropic, grieving acquaintance. She asked me out for coffee to see how I was doing. She knew intimately and tragically what it felt like to lose a son. Her boy died in his sophomore year of high school from suicide.

She told me that she and her husband would like to make a donation to a charity of Hughdad's and my choosing, in honor of our boy. Or, if we preferred, they could seed a charitable fund that we would administer, and donate to different organizations in Hugh's name. That so touched and overwhelmed me. I mentioned earlier that I was inspired by Stephen Jenkinson's talk during the Shift Network's Beyond the Veil Summit to make sure Hugh is never forgotten—and wanted to get activated to do good works in his name—but husband Hugh and I hadn't figured that out yet.

She told me that a friend of theirs seeded a charitable fund when her boy died, and how that all worked. I told her I wanted to talk with Hughdad about this and what would work best. We loved the idea of a fund, but also acknowledged the huge responsibility of researching, finding the right organizations that our boy would be so proud to be a part of, engaging with them, being the shepherds of this generous gift. We were so honored by this offer and gratefully accepted.

It took a few months of exploration to eventually set that up through a Schwab Charitable donor-advised fund. Our financial advisor scheduled meetings with us and the Schwab Charitable administrator, and we talked through how to set this up. We had no idea how much our acquaintance planned to donate, and we were too timid to ask because we were grateful for *any* amount. The day came when the Hugh Saffel Charitable Fund was all set up, and the donation came in. We were stunned and moved by the generosity of the donation. And now responsible for shepherding that.

At the end of Hugh's celebration of life, I spoke about the talk I watched by the therapist who has worked for decades in the hospice environment with thousands of people at the end of their lives. He said the thing that surprised him most is that of all the things there are to think about at the end of life, people are most afraid of being forgotten by those they love. That was very poignant to me. I asked that people never forget Hugh. To speak of him. Speak *to* him. Tell stories about him. And that through a generous donation and the creation of the Hugh Saffel Charitable Fund, we would do good works in the community in Hugh's name. I asked that if anyone had ideas about organizations that seemed like something Hugh would be passionate about, to let us know—and that, somehow, funding access to basketball programs for all is definitely something that came to our minds.

Two friends reached out to us with an idea. Their son was super involved with youth baseball, and they knew of an incredible organization called Baseball Beyond Borders, whose mission it is to level the playing field of baseball one community at a time and to help student athletes of color connect their passion for baseball with their academic futures off the field. They thought the founder might know of an equivalent basketball program, so they connected us to him.

Indeed, the founder—one of the most dynamic, engaging, brilliant people—knew just who we should talk with. He was on the board of a new organization called the Give Back Foundation, started by eighteen-year-old elite Seattle basketball player Nolan Hickman Jr., who was now a starter for college basketball powerhouse Gonzaga University.

Nolan, who has always been a doer and a giver, started the foundation to transform the health and wellness of youth by providing families with the necessary resources meant to make meaningful and lasting change—and to create an inclusive environment for youth to thrive in life, sports, and leadership. The foundation is involved with many initiatives, such as providing school supplies, supporting health and nutrition initiatives, and funding sports scholarships.

Being the basketball player that he is, Nolan also puts on a basketball camp once a year in underserved communities, providing an opportunity for boys and girls, ages eight to thirteen, to play and be mentored by wonderful young coaches—gaining skills, confidence, and fitness.

Two years after Hugh passed, husband Hugh and I met with the foundation's board, loved them, and felt it was a great match for what Hugh would be passionate about. We easily decided to put funding toward supporting the camp. During the course of the conversations, we told the board all about Hugh's passion for the game, and that he sometimes wasn't the best player but that he loved it so much and put 1,000 percent of himself into it, leaving everything out on the court. As plans progressed for our participation, the board told us that they decided to give the Hugh Saffel Heart of the Game Award to one child in each age bracket for those who exhibited that same passion for the game. Man, that was a lot to take in. We were so emotional and beyond grateful to have our boy honored in that way. They even promoted it on social media in the lead-up to the camp.

The photo used to promote the Hugh Saffel Heart of the Game Award.

The people of the foundation are just the best—many are Nolan's family—and on the day of the camp, when we arrived, they gave us the Give Back Foundation T-shirts and special beaded bracelets and wouldn't let us do any work. It brought us such joy being back on a basketball court, hearing the bouncing balls, squeaking shoes, scoreboard buzzers, all of which we had missed so much. All of which were programmed into our bodies, minds, and souls.

In each of the two age brackets, there was a child who caught our eye and reminded us so much of Hugh and the way he played, and how much he loved the game. We had nothing to do with determining which child would receive the Hugh Saffel Heart of the Game Award, but wouldn't you know, those were the same kids who caught Nolan's eye as well and who received the award. I just knew Hugh was there watching, loving it so much, and being so proud to be a part of it. And for me, the camp was the first time I'd felt pure joy since Hugh passed. My heart was lifted, and I didn't want it to end. It opened my eyes to how joy and grief can coexist and started my thinking of wanting to choose happiness and to live my best life because I knew Hugh was watching me, too, and I want him to be proud of me as well.

16

WHY DID HUGH
HAVE TO LEAVE?

As elated as I felt with all the beautiful teachings and connections I was experiencing with mediumship, it didn't protect me from going through crippling grief bombs. I was
almost three years into this journey, and I still had questions and still felt that my heart was torn asunder on any
given day.

A lot of people believe everything happens for a reason.
In light of the horrific things that happen in the world, I
have always questioned that philosophy, and wondered if
things happen for a reason or if they just happen. It seems to
be a common thing to say to someone who has lost a loved
one: "God doesn't make mistakes. Everything happens for
a reason." As if that will somehow evoke comfort. It's such
a good thing no one has ever said that to me in the tragedy
of my son's death. Because I would have been pissed. What

reason could it possibly be that a bright, hopeful, young life ends far too soon, leaving the rest of us with grief and trauma in its wake?

As I've gone on this spiritual journey with many top-notch teachers, there has been much discussion about the soul and our unique soul's journey. It is said that our soul reincarnates into this life to learn very specific lessons—things that have been missing in our soul's countless other lifetimes. And reincarnating into a human form is but one of the choices a soul has, albeit a very popular one because life on earth is the best school there is. With our soul's journey comes agreements with other souls to be catalysts for what the other needs to learn. That is all way above my pay grade to understand.

Ever since Hugh passed, I found myself taking classes and going to practitioners, both things I would never have fathomed doing before. A dear friend of mine who lost her daughter in an accident and is on a spiritual journey as well told me about seeing a woman who does Akashic readings and how she had a deeply powerful and enlightening experience. So I decided to go, too.

The Akashic Records are said to be the record of our entire soul's journey, past, present, and future. According to the website of the practitioner I went to, "the Akashic Realm is a dimension of consciousness that holds a vibrational record of every soul and its journey throughout time as a human. By accessing the Records, we are able to receive information on your path from a soul perspective. In a reading, we explore who you truly are and get guidance on overcoming any limitations in aligning with that truth in this lifetime. In this knowledge, you can be empowered to heal." In a reading, your masters, spirit guides, and/or loved ones come through with infinite knowledge and wisdom about your soul.

It doesn't get more woo-woo than that, but I was game. With Hugh's death, my life had become everything before that moment and then everything after. And I was really struggling with the everything that comes after. Ever since my friend told me about the Akashic Records reading, I was vitalized by the opportunity for more learning. For me, learning, learning, and more learning seemed to be my way through my struggles and sometimes overwhelming grief.

Tracie, the healer who did my reading, was a beautiful person inside and out, with curly red hair piled atop her head like a medieval goddess. I spent an hour in the reading and fortunately recorded the session on my phone. There was so much. So, so much I would never have remembered. She said she was connecting with my masters and loved ones. She was told I came to this world to explore being a caregiver, and man, does that fit. That has come up over and over in my life. And honestly, I'm so tired of it. I would like to check that off my soul's list and move on. It came up repeatedly in the reading that I need to anchor in self-care before I'm ready for what comes next—and there's a lot coming.

Without knowing anything about me, Tracie said the

masters were showing her that I am here to help people manage grief through a spiritual connection and to hold space for other people in their process. What I've gleaned in my process has apparently become part of my medicine to help others. Tracie even asked if I lead support groups. (Yes, I told her I do through Helping Parents Heal, which I will talk more about later.) "And does the support group have an element of spirituality? (Yes, it does.) This is the gift. This is going to be part of your path, because you're healing with this, but don't underestimate the ripple effect of how it will help others. Keep showing up in this lane."

She gave me highly specific information about my path that felt right. And about my day job and how it will intersect with my life's real purpose. And about how my mind, which I see as a foe, is essential in this path. I got solid insight into what is blocking my intuitive gifts. She even referenced a need for my husband and me to take a vacation together, which we had just been talking about that morning. She said, "I don't know why they're bringing this in, but has it been hard to take a family trip since this all happened? It's time. They're showing me that it's important to take one-on-one time with just your husband, then with your child. This is an important part of your healing to open the door and let some light in."

And then I got to ask questions. I felt a welling up of emotion deep inside me, and I choked out, "Why did Hugh have to leave so soon?"

With great compassion, Tracie told me:

"They show that Hugh had explored what he wanted to. There is a sense of, on a soul level, he'd gotten what he needed and wanted to do this differently. It was a quick turn in another direction. A course correct."

Tracie asked, "Can I bring in a message? (Of course.) What your guides want is for you to know that this is an event to provide freedom in your life and not be shackled by grief.

"This was meant to be a catalyst to really expand you, and while it feels very raw and heavy, it's meant to liberate you. That's what Hugh really wants—is to honor him by creating a bigger, broader life for yourself.

"He keeps coming through, encouraging you to 'do something for yourself, Mom. You're always worried about us.' He's OK. He wants this to open up freedom for you. Freedom to explore what you want to do and not feel like you have to take care of everyone all the time.

"This of course rocked the whole dynamics of the family. And also brought you closer together.

"They're showing that it's an opportunity to learn what you can extract from life.

"Did Hugh march to the beat of his own drum? (Yes.) They're showing that this life just didn't fit for Hugh. On a soul level, he was like, 'OK, I've done this. I'm ready to do something different.' This was a liberation for him, but he doesn't want it to shackle the rest of you. He wants this to liberate you. The biggest gift you can give him is to allow yourself to feel the freedom.

"It's hard to make sense of why our soul would choose these things. But just think, it's a continuation on in a different direction. He made a choice to do something different. How it shows up on your path is a real awakening and opening to what's important and what lies beyond. Cultivating that sense of direction.

"Hugh and your team want you to explore levity and lightheartedness. In this heavy time, it's time to open a door to let them take some heaviness and burden off of you. You don't need to be mired all the time. You can show others that you're evolving your relationship with grief and with your loved ones as you navigate this path. You came here to experience that navigation so that you can also share that with other people."

And so I am.

Perhaps the things that happen in our lives are not random acts. Perhaps they truly are all designed for what our soul needs to learn. That's been a bit of a bitter pill for me to swallow in my grief. But I feel that possibility opening up in me.

17

OF MY SOUL,
NOT MY DNA

Hugh made me a mother, and for that, I am eternally grateful. For millions of people, having a child—something so natural, so deeply personal, and so profoundly desired—is not something you can just make happen. Our road to parenthood was longer than that of many. Shorter than others'. After having a heartbreaking miscarriage and experiencing infertility, we had testing done, which showed there was a little something on my side and a little something on Hughdad's side contributing to the infertility. We decided to have medical science help us to a certain point, but weren't interested in going the route of extensive interventions. Over time, we agreed that there is absolutely nothing special about our DNA, and that we would be honored to shepherd someone else's. We arrived easily at the idea of adoption. We trusted that if we were meant to be parents, we would have the child we were supposed to have.

In my usual research fashion, I looked into a lot of adoption agencies and went to informational meetings. We fell in love with an agency called New Hope, which sadly no longer exists because so many adoption connections are now made through the internet. The way the adoptions worked through New Hope is that the birthmothers received a tremendous amount of support of all kinds through the agency, and the decision about the home the baby got placed in was one made by the birthmother. Around the eighth month of pregnancy, the birthmothers were given portfolios of prospective parents to choose from, then they got to meet the parents they'd chosen to make sure the birthmother felt great and right about her choice. The correct terminology to use around adoption is that the birthmother makes an adoption plan for her baby—not that she's giving her baby up for adoption. It is an act of love for a birthmother to make this decision if she's not in the position to parent. There can be tremendous grief for birthmothers around the decision, not only for her but also for her extended family.

Admittedly, Hughdad and I had a pretty good portfolio. We are both marketing professionals, and we had a designer friend visually create the story of us that we wrote, with a lot of photos of our adventures and the life we cherish together. You never know what a birthmother is looking for. She may want the adoptive parents to practice a certain religion. Or live in the city, or the country. Or for this to be the first child in the family, or to have ready-made siblings. Or any number of things. Hugh's birthmother Nicole said that she liked the fact that we had been stable and married a long time—seven years at that point—and were physically active and traveled a lot. Those were things she valued.

Before we even got to the portfolio stage, we had a rigorous evaluation. We had to go through marriage counseling sessions as well as group sessions with other prospective parents. We had to submit to a full financial assessment to make sure we could support a child. The agency did a home visit to confirm that we had a safe home to raise a child in. We had to have physicals. And it required letters of reference. When you adopt a child, you really know that you want to be parents because there are no blessed accidents here. Many mediums and spiritualists say that we pick our parents. If that's the case, Hugh really made us jump through a lot of hoops to be his parents—maybe to see if we had what it takes to handle everything that was going to be coming.

I have wondered, if we pick our parents, why would anyone pick parents who end up being abusive or neglectful, or are in any situation of war, poverty, or distress. And if our soul determines what it wants to learn in this lifetime— which is also a widely held notion—why would anyone choose addiction, disease, mental illness, trauma? I've been told that there is the soul's journey and there is the human's journey, and that we can't possibly understand from the human perspective what the soul's journey is. That it will be understood by us only after we cross over.

It was nerve racking knowing our portfolio was out for

review, along with others. Your portfolio isn't given to all birthmothers, just the ones with whom you match with what they're looking for. It was about six months of regular check-ins with the agency before we got that phone call from them saying we had been selected by a birthmother who was due in five weeks—and we were scheduled to meet her in two. It was an indescribably joyous phone call—very much like finding out you're pregnant, but also different because of all the work we had put into it, and because it was something completely out of our hands. Someone else was making the decision for us.

Nicole was attending college in another state. We have so much respect and admiration for her in all ways, one of which is that it must have been so hard being pregnant and giving birth just three months into her first freshman semester. She was a strong, smart young woman and an accomplished student and athlete, and she carried this all off with tremendous grace. We flew in, and you can well imagine the nervousness we felt walking into the Italian restaurant to meet her, her best friend, and the New Hope counselor. It was the biggest, most important audition of our lives.

It ended up that she was just as nervous as we were. But it was all so easy. We hit it off and talked like old friends. The thing that hit me when Hughdad and I walked in and I saw Hugh's birthmother was how much she and I look alike. We took photos together, and I look at them again now, and it's uncanny. We have the exact same strong lower jawline and face shape. I look just like an older, brunette version of her. I wondered if that might have played into her decision, consciously or subconsciously. Maybe she thought that I might look a bit like her child, which people told me I did. The meeting went really well, and we were on cloud nine after meeting her.

But we had one more audition. We were also meeting Hugh's birthfather, Matt, the next day at the adoption agency's office. He drove in from an adjacent state to meet us, with his parents. He had told his parents only two days before that he had fathered a child, soon to be born. A bomb dropped on their household that day, and I have so much compassion for them when their world got turned upside down in that moment. They had absolutely no idea. Their son and Nicole had not really been in a relationship, as far as they knew. His parents were bewildered, and also didn't want to assume that the child was going to be adopted. Matt had an older sister with two young children, and they all wondered if the sister could raise the baby. I know it was such a shock and it was moving so fast that they didn't even have a chance to talk about it and be involved in any decisions. Matt was a great kid, you could tell. And a tall, handsome star of the high school basketball team with a family that was so lovely and kind. Our joy was tempered by the grief we knew the two families were feeling.

There's a whole lot of story between here and when we held that beautiful baby in our arms when he was just an hour and a half old. Stories of adoption laws in that state and more hoops to go through. Stories of us going back home after meeting Hugh's birthparents and praying that everything was still going to work out. Stories of the call that changed our lives: Nicole was being induced the next day, and we needed to get on a plane.

There are also stories of Seattle being under siege and our uncertainty if we could even catch a flight out. Forty thousand people were rioting in Seattle—now known as the Battle of Seattle—when the World Trade Organization Ministerial Conference convened in the city and protesters fought for workers' rights, sustainable economies, and environmental and social issues. It became anarchy, and the city felt like a smoke-filled war zone. It was a miracle we were able to book a flight with a moment's notice and go meet our boy.

And there are stories of the first moment we saw our son. I don't know what it's like to look into the eyes of a child you created, but I can tell you I couldn't possibly love that boy more in his twenty years of life as his adoptive mother. He is my beating heart.

We've had people point out that we've had a lot of challenges with our adopted children. And that when you adopt, you don't know what you're getting. Yeah, well, guess what, you also don't know what you're getting when you give birth to your children. We have many friends who have equal or greater challenges with their biological children. No matter how a child comes into your life, it's going to be a wild roller-coaster ride.

I harken back to the 1989 movie *Parenthood* when Gil

and Karen find out they are unexpectedly pregnant with their fourth child. Gil freaks out with all the reasons why this isn't a great thing. Karen counters by telling him that life is messy and that she loves the mess. Gil's darling, aged grandmother overhears and comes out from the kitchen to say:

"You know, when I was nineteen, Grandpa took me on a roller coaster. Up, down, up, down. Oh, what a ride! I always wanted to go again. You know, it was just so interesting to me that a ride could make me so frightened, so scared, so sick, so excited, and so thrilled all together! Some didn't like it. They went on the merry-go-round. That just goes around. Nothing. I like the roller coaster. You get more out of it."

And she walks away.

We certainly did go on a ride with our boy. I now wish I had loved the messiness more and leaned into the chaos and uncertainty, savoring every second, joyous or difficult, because that's what we had with the boy who chose us.

Opposite: "Downtown Seattle became a city under lockdown today as Seattle police—in a much tougher stance than yesterday's—began arresting hundreds of protesters who ventured inside a zone of more than 50 blocks that was declared off-limits to demonstrations for the remainder of the World Trade Organization conference." The Seattle Times front page on December 1, 1999, the day Hugh was born.

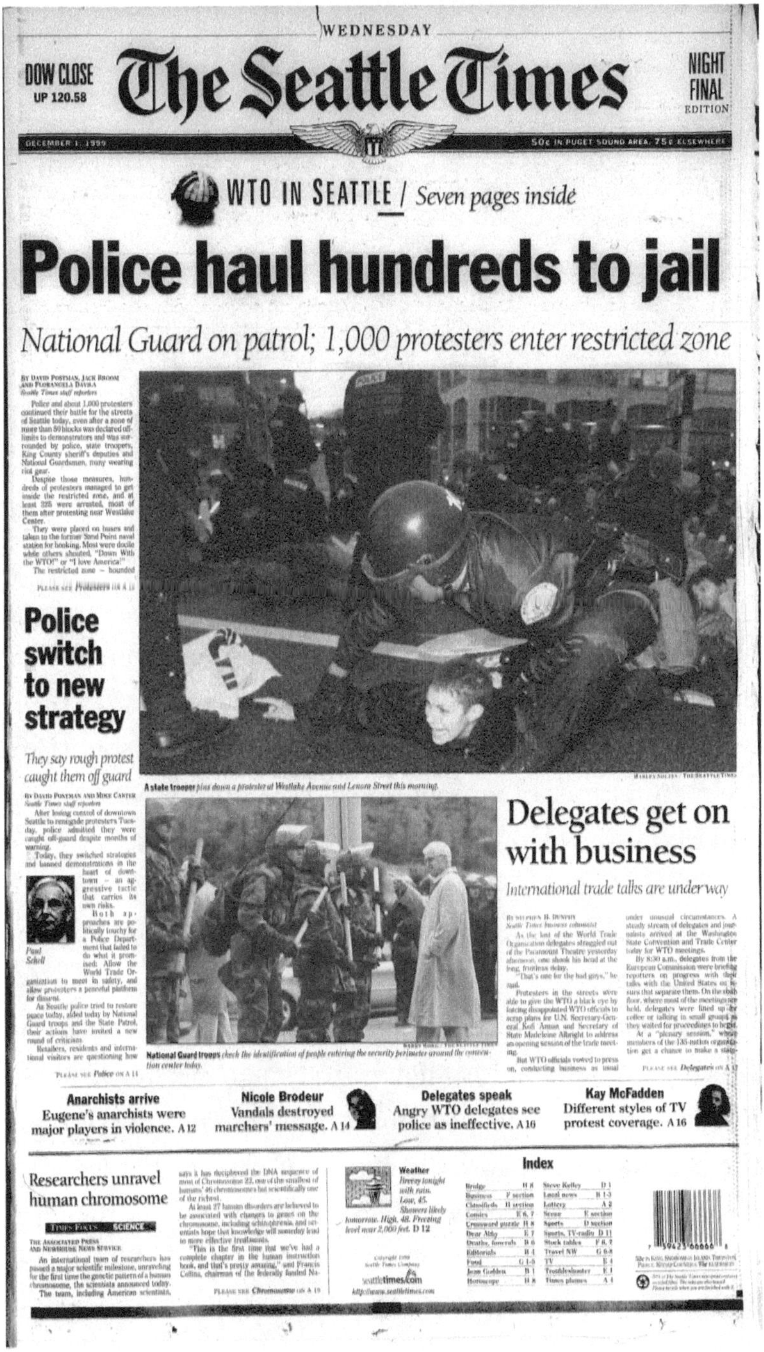

WEDNESDAY

DOW CLOSE UP 120.58

The Seattle Times

NIGHT FINAL EDITION

DECEMBER 1, 1999   50¢ IN PUGET SOUND AREA, 75¢ ELSEWHERE

WTO IN SEATTLE / *Seven pages inside*

Police haul hundreds to jail

National Guard on patrol; 1,000 protesters enter restricted zone

BY DAVID POSTMAN, JACK BROOM
AND FLORANGELA DAVILA
Seattle Times staff reporters

Police and about 1,000 protesters continued their battle for the streets of Seattle today, even after a zone of more than 80 blocks was declared off-limits to demonstrations and was surrounded by police, state troopers, King County sheriff's deputies and National Guardsmen, many wearing riot gear.

Despite those measures, hundreds of protesters managed to get inside the restricted zone, and at least 335 were arrested, most of them after protesting near Westlake Center.

They were placed on buses and taken to the former Sand Point naval station for booking. Most were docile while others shouted, "Down With the WTO!" or "I love America."

The restricted zone — bounded

PLEASE SEE Protesters ON A 13

Police switch to new strategy

They say rough protest caught them off guard

BY DAVID POSTMAN AND MIKE CARTER
Seattle Times staff reporters

After losing control of downtown Seattle to renegade protesters Tuesday, police admitted they were caught off-guard despite months of warning.

Today, they switched strategies and banned demonstrations in the heart of downtown — an aggressive tactic that carries its own risks.

Both approaches are politically touchy for a Police Department that failed to do what it promised: Allow the World Trade Organization to meet in safety, and allow protesters a peaceful platform for dissent.

An Seattle police tried to restore peace today, aided today by National Guard troops and the State Patrol, their actions have invited a new round of criticism.

Retailers, residents and international visitors are questioning how

PLEASE SEE Police ON A 11

Paul Scholl

A state trooper pins down a protester at Westlake Avenue and Lenora Street this morning. HARLEY SOLTES · THE SEATTLE TIMES

National Guard troops check the identification of people entering the security perimeter around the convention center today. HARRY WONG · FOR THE SEATTLE TIMES

Delegates get on with business

International trade talks are under way

BY STEPHEN H. DUNPHY
Seattle Times business columnist

As the last of the World Trade Organization delegates struggled out of the Paramount Theatre yesterday afternoon, one shook his head at the long, fruitless delay.

"That's one for the bad guys," he said.

Protesters in the streets were able to give the WTO a black eye by forcing disappointed WTO officials to scrap plans for U.N. Secretary-General Kofi Annan and Secretary of State Madeleine Albright to address an opening session of the trade meeting.

But WTO officials vowed to press on, conducting business as usual

under unusual circumstances. A steady stream of delegates and journalists arrived at the Washington State Convention and Trade Center today for WTO meetings.

By 8:30 a.m. delegates from the European Commission were briefing reporters on progress with their talks with the United States on issues that separate them. On the sixth floor, where most of the meetings are held, delegates were lined up for coffee or talking in small groups as they waited for proceedings to begin.

At a "plenary session," where members of the 135-nation organization get a chance to make a state-

PLEASE SEE Delegates ON A 12

Anarchists arrive	**Nicole Brodeur**	**Delegates speak**	**Kay McFadden**
Eugene's anarchists were major players in violence. A 12	Vandals destroyed marchers' message. A 14	Angry WTO delegates see police as ineffective. A 16	Different styles of TV protest coverage. A 16

Researchers unravel human chromosome

TIMES · FOCUS **SCIENCE**

THE ASSOCIATED PRESS
AND NEWHOUSE NEWS SERVICE

An international team of researchers has passed a major scientific milestone, unraveling for the first time the genetic pattern of a human chromosome, the scientists announced today.

The team, including American scientists,

says it has deciphered the DNA sequence of most of Chromosome 22, one of the smallest of humans' 46 chromosomes but scientifically one of the richest.

At least 27 human disorders are believed to be associated with changes to genes on the chromosome, including schizophrenia, and scientists hope that knowledge will someday lead to more effective treatments.

"This is the first time that we've had a complete chapter in the human instruction book, and that's pretty amazing," said Francis Collins, chairman of the federally funded Na-

PLEASE SEE Chromosome ON A 19

Weather
Breezy tonight with rain. Low, 45. Showers likely tomorrow. High, 48. Freezing level near 3,000 feet. D 12

Index

Bridge	H 8	Steve Kelley	D 1
Business	F section	Local news	B 1-3
Classifieds	H section	Lottery	A 2
Comics	E 6, 7	Scene	E section
Crossword puzzle	H 8	Sports	D section
Dear Abby	E 7	Sports, TV-radio	D 11
Deaths, burials	B 6	Stock tables	F 4, 5
Editorials	B 4	Travel NW	G 6-8
Food	G 1-4	TV	E 6
Jean Godden	B 1	Troubleshooter	E 1
Horoscope	H 8	Times planes	A 4

Copyright 1999
Seattle Times Company

seattletimes.com
http://www.seattletimes.com

18

THREE FAMILIES
FOREVER BOUND

Many people have asked if we told Hugh's birthparents that he passed away. The answer is: Yes, of course. Just as there were many stories of how Hugh came to be our son, there are many stories of our continued relationship with Nicole and Matt—the birthparents, who Hugh also chose.

After Hugh was born, we couldn't leave the state until the paperwork cleared both their and Washington's adoption protocols. And we weren't allowed to have Hugh for seventy-two hours after his birth—a nail-biting time during which a birthmother is allowed to change her mind about making an adoption plan for her baby—so after leaving the hospital, Hugh stayed a couple of days with a wonderful family that worked with the adoption agency. They had five daughters and were delighted to have a baby boy in the house. Hugh even went to a *Nutcracker* ballet rehearsal one of the girls was in when he was just two days old! They were a wonderful family, and we got to hang out there with them and Hugh. After Hugh was released to us, we stayed in a hotel for two weeks, waiting for the paperwork to clear so we could fly back to Seattle. It was longer than usual due to it being the holiday season, and it was strange to start our life as a family in a hotel.

We had a contract with Hugh's birthparents through the adoption agency until he was eighteen years old. It required that once a year, we send a letter with photos to each birthparent. This would be considered a semi-open adoption, as we didn't know each other's last names or addresses, and all correspondence went through the agency, which they would forward. We also had an additional requirement with Matt that we would bring Hugh to visit sometime in his first year—a clause that more likely came from his parents than from Matt. We flew there when Hugh was nine months old and spent a beautiful day with Matt and his family. I can't imagine what it was like for a teenaged boy to be met with this visit. There was fear in his eyes, and I really felt for him. Thankfully, he had a friend over to offer him support. This was certainly his life playing out in ways he would never have expected, and making the best of it.

Over those years, communication was mostly one-way, with us sending the letters—although Matt's mom stayed in touch, sending us childhood pictures and newspaper clippings about Matt's games. The letters from Nicole started to be returned to the adoption agency as undeliverable, something we felt very sad about. We assumed she had moved on and hadn't left a forwarding address.

The agency counseled adoptive parents to be open with the child about their adoption from day one. There should never be the Big Momentous Day when a person finds out they were adopted and perhaps feels like their life has been a lie. This is very different from days of old—when there was often family secrecy around adoption, and adoption records were sealed to protect the identity of the birthmother— and certainly is a much healthier approach. We were further counseled on all the correct language to use, such as that our child *was* adopted, not *is* adopted. Adoption isn't a person's identity; it's how we came to be a family. So, we had pictures of Hugh's birthparents around, talked about them, told him his story, and told him that if he ever wanted more information about them or was interested in meeting them, we would be so happy to reach out to them. He actually didn't seem interested in it or like he spent much time thinking about it.

But, right when Hugh turned twenty, with the power of the internet, it took one of Hugh's birth cousins exactly a nanosecond to find him on social media. Matt's family knew we lived in Seattle and knew our first names of course, so I mean, duh, they were able to find our last name just like magic. Then it was easy to track down the younger Hugh Saffel on social media. I am now deeply grateful that happened. It was just a few months before Hugh passed away. Hugh was open with his cousin about his addiction, and she connected him to Matt. We came to find out that Matt himself had a ten-year opioid addiction starting when he, too, was twenty. He told Hugh that he found his way through it with intense exercise, and Hugh was inspired to go down that path, too. He was starting to get really fit. And things were looking up.

Recovery was apparently not meant to be. Just as Hugh seemed to be turning a corner and we had great days together, he made an impulsive and fatal choice. Then, the unfortunate thing with social media happened when the mother of one of Hugh's closest friends posted about Hugh's death on Facebook. However the Facebook algorithms work, Matt's mom—who had started following Hugh on Facebook—got that post in her feed from someone she didn't even know. Oh, that was bad. So, so bad. That's not the way we would want anyone in the inner circle to find out. She called us in a panic. We hadn't had a chance to notify the birth families yet. We were heartsick about how that played out.

I was so worried they would think we hadn't been good parents, or hadn't done absolutely everything we could to help Hugh, or were somehow at fault. But that was not at all what happened. I think because of Matt's own addiction and how his family suffered, helpless, through that, they wrapped us in love. Matt's addiction was decades ago, before fentanyl arrived on the scene, when opioid addiction was wretched and life ruining, but not as lethal. We had a beautiful phone call with Matt where we told him we knew of no way to reach Nicole. He and Nicole were connected on social media, so he got a message through to her, and she called us.

Oh, that was such a hard phone call. With the woman who birthed our son, who we hadn't talked to since. One of the greatest sadnesses of that conversation was learning that she said she had always wanted to meet Hugh but had stopped receiving our letters and thought we didn't want contact. That was the furthest thing from our wishes, and we were both bewildered why the letters to her were returned to the agency as undeliverable, and the agency, in turn, sent them back to us. She'd had her parents' address listed as the contact, and that hadn't changed. I had kept all the letters that were returned and sent them to her. It was some consolation, but there had been a huge error somewhere along the way that led to a very sorrowful missed opportunity.

We included mention of Hugh's birth family—who he had recently connected with—in his obituary. And we invited them to his celebration of life. We also live-streamed the event for those who lived far and wide or were uncomfortable with a gathering. Hugh's birth family attended online, from various states.

So here we are, a few years down the road, still in touch. Matt's sister contacted me and asked if I had any of Hugh's basketball jerseys to spare that she could have. She knew someone who makes bears wearing the jerseys, and she wanted to have one made for Matt. The one I sent her was a double-sided jersey, so she had one made for us, too. A blond, blue-eyed bear wearing Hugh's Seattle Parks and

Recreation jersey, with a red heart-shaped patch with "Hugh IV" on the sole of the foot. We all text each other on Hugh's birthday and angel date.

I know we will be connected forever, those people whose beautiful DNA created our son, and us, who lovingly raised him to twenty. When I think of the soul's journey, I know we were meant to know one another—for what reasons, I don't know. I now picture the soul connections of all those in our lives like a big Hoberman sphere—one of those children's toys with many joints that you can pull outward to expand into a gigantic ball, exposing all the different points of connection and the cords between them. Each point dependent on the other to support the beautiful creation. I am grateful for these good people and the journey we're on together, tragic as it is.

19

WAS, IS, AND WILL ALWAYS BE

When I was writing about Hugh's adoption and went through his things to retrieve the adoption scrapbook I made for him—to remind myself of the magic and emotion of the process of being selected by his birthmother, of meeting his birthparents, of his birth—I came across a folded, crumply letter I had written to Hugh in high school and didn't know he had saved. I had written the letter at the request of his school when all the seniors were going on a four-day retreat, and parents were asked to write a letter of love, support, and encouragement for our kids. In the Catholic school system, that's called a palanca letter—a religious practice of sending blessings to a loved one.

Going through Hugh's things at any time and for any reason is so hard for me to this day. When he passed, it wasn't an option to leave his room exactly as is, as a time capsule of his physical life. This was right at the beginning of the pandemic, and my company turned to 100 percent remote work. I needed an office in the house with a desk large enough for three computers and two monitors, a filing cabinet, a printer, an office chair. We needed Hugh's room to be a multipurpose room—this room where he died.

His bed is still in the room, and it took me months to stop feeling the dread of seeing that huge elephant in the room every day. It carried a heavy, tragic energy. I had never done anything like this before, but I burned sage and ceremoniously whisked any bad energy out the open window. There is a dresser with six huge drawers, now filled to the brim with the things essential to keep: Hugh's basketball jerseys and all his caps, his phone and wallet, his cologne and hair gel, his favorite camouflage water bottle, the backstage pass to see Chance the Rapper, love letters from his girlfriend, the nubby rubber balls he had in his hand or at his foot 24-7, souvenirs, gifts from friends, school papers, childhood drawings, photo albums. And his ashes. His entire physical being reduced to eight and a half pounds of ash in a black box. I've noticed that my heart rate always increases when I need to go into those drawers, or into the closet where his favorite clothes and shoes remain.

It was a happy thing to find the letter I had written ahead of Hugh's senior-year retreat. The retreat was called Kairos, translated from ancient Greek as "God's time," and is an opportunity for students to strengthen their relationship with God and the cohort community through openness, trust, and reflection. I remember Hugh came back changed, having bared his soul to his peers—as they all had. There was a lightness, an ease in him that he had been 100 percent himself, laid it all out there, and had been wholly accepted as he is.

In my letter, I typed:

> Dear Hugh,
>
> It is such a joy and an honor to be your mom and to witness you becoming who you are. From the tow-headed little boy with an internal engine that never slowed—and who always had a ball in his hand—to the fun young man who is kind and thoughtful—and who always has a ball in his hand—you have impressed me. Entertained me. Challenged me. Given me purpose.
>
> Every year since you were born, I've done some journaling about who you are and about the milestones in your life. I just now read all of that over again, and it was really poignant to realize that there are so many of your beautiful qualities that you've had from the very beginning.
>
> When you were just eleven months old, I wrote, "It's probably too early to tell what Hugh's personality will be, but right now, he is confident, social, expressive, and a bit of a daredevil. In a group of babies, he's

always the one to dive head first into a bin of toys, with his legs sticking straight up in the air, or to climb up and over an obstacle rather than go around it."

Life has been filled with plenty of obstacles, lots of things that aren't easy, but you've always gone up and over them, Hugh. You've handled them head-on with grace, and that internal engine of yours just keeps going. Because of that, I have great confidence that you can handle whatever comes your way.

When you were four years old, I wrote, "Hugh is very strong willed and has a lot of ideas of his own. He doesn't very often just do what someone asks him to do. He's a master negotiator. He'll start the negotiation with the phrase 'Let me tell you something,' and then will proceed to bargain to get five more minutes on the playground, or one more cookie. He keeps us on our toes."

Believe me, there have been countless times over the last eighteen years when I've wished you'd just do what Dad and I ask you to do. That would have been so much easier. But that's not who you are. And because of that, I have great confidence that no one is going to push you around and that you won't just take the easy way out. You'll do what's right.

When you were five, I wrote, "Hugh's teachers say that he puts a lot of energy into being a good friend and is very empathetic. He's apparently really good at conflict resolution, too, although I must say we don't see much of that at home with his little brother!"

As I read back over all the years' writings, the thing that comes up over and over and over is how important your friends are to you. I know you'd agree with me now that they are the most important thing to you. Just as you've gone through challenges, so have your friends, and you've been there for them. Because of that, I have great confidence that you will never be alone.

When you were eight, I wrote, "Hugh's friends' parents all comment on what a pleasure it is to have him over at their houses. He's respectful, looks adults in the eye and converses with them, and is great with the younger brothers and sisters."

You've always been intuitive about what's going on with people, and you're easy to talk to, and you express yourself well. I've read many times that one of the key factors in success is having good social skills—more so than academic skills—and you have social skills in abundance. Because of that, I have great confidence that people will think highly of you and will give you opportunities.

When you were nine, I wrote, "Hugh still plays soccer and basketball, he skis and skateboards and is willing to try just about any sport or any activity. We love his attitude."

You have always been game. For just about anything. As you've gotten older, that has translated to a love of travel, and you've already gotten to go to a lot of fascinating places in your young years. Because of that, I have great confidence that your life will be interesting and full of adventure.

Let's jump to you at seventeen, when I wrote, "Hugh's interests are still sports and friends. Friends and sports. Sports. Friends. Oh, and candy and TV to watch all the sports. With his friends. And more sports."

Well, there's nothing more to say there!

Hugh, I know that in your senior year, as you try to figure out your next move after high school, the future is filled with uncertainty. Don't worry. You have everything it takes to be successful, to maneuver a winding path and still get to the top of the mountain. And you will always have Dad and I beside you, being your biggest fans, lifting you up, and loving you more and more every day.

Your very lucky mom,

Wendy

I'm gutted that things didn't work out for Hugh the way anyone would hope for. None of us had any idea what was on the horizon. Things felt so good and so hopeful at that moment.

But the joy I find in this letter is in looking at some little snapshots of his life and realizing that who he was at age one was who he was till age twenty. In the nature versus nurture debate, as an adoptive parent, I initially planted a flag on the side of nurture and environment having the greatest influence on who we become. No doubt, that's massively influential, and the science known as epigenetics shows that environment and behaviors can actually change the way our genes work. At the same time, I've experienced with my kids that we all come out of the chute hardwired with personalities, ways of processing information, gifts and propensities, and certainly our physicality. Nature and nurture come together to make each of us the unique, no-one-else-like-us-on-earth person we are.

What I find most remarkable now is that in evidence-based mediumship readings, the medium first establishes that your loved one is there by relaying those distinguishable characteristics. This gives you the confidence and relief that your person is really there.

Hugh's appearance is occasionally described—tall, athletic, light-brown hair parted on the side, with bangs swept across his forehead. His *essence* is always described similarly from medium to medium—adventurous and risk-taking, strong willed, very social, well liked, high energy, funny, emotionally intelligent, likes balls and sports. All true, true, true. Since he was a wee lad. And now as I can connect with Hugh some on my own, I get his sass as well.

When I found the letter in Hugh's messy drawer, and read it with the same poignance that I wrote it with, I thought about how much it relates to my experiences with who he is on the Other Side. Even though Hugh's physical being is no longer here, he is still the same person I have always loved. And he will always be.

20

WHY ME?

Even though I was able to put Hugh's birth, his life, his passing, and now his afterlife into a beautiful and comforting spiritual context, on any given day, I can still throw a really fine pity party. Even now, as I type these words, I just can't believe this tragedy happened to Hugh. To me. To our family. My learning is showing me that perhaps it is a part of our souls' plans, but that doesn't mean I like it. I occasionally have conversations with my soul where I say, "Thanks a lot. I may be experiencing things that advance you, but I have a human mind and a human heart, and my heart is broken."

I subscribe to Suzanne Giesemann's newsletter *Living the Awakened Way*. She is a person who is really tapped into spiritual masters, which she collectively calls Sanaya, and through a meditative writing practice is able to channel their wisdom and download brilliant insights. In one of her newsletters, she printed the answer that she received to a question she asked the masters:

Was suffering part of my soul's plan?

Sanaya: "'Why do some face more challenges than others?' you ask. It is because they can handle it, and more will be the growth of those around them for it. These special souls did enter this life agreeing to take on more than their share, for they realized what lessons in love these challenges would be. It is the nature of the human being to forget these agreements when you dress in a body, but the spirit knows that all challenges are opportunities for the growth of many, not just the one. When you pass from the body, you will see how intricately it all fits together and what an important role your challenges played in the growth of many souls. How one handles challenges depends greatly on one's perception. It is always a choice to view a challenge as a tragedy or an opportunity. Step back from your human reaction, and see with the eyes of spirit. Rather than sinking into the depths of despair, flood all situations with love, then rise to the surface and breathe."

I have always appreciated when people are candid about the challenges of their lives and don't create a picture of social media perfection. It allows us to see ourselves in those hardships, build empathy for others, and know that we're not alone—we're on a shared journey through this life, and absolutely, our experiences can help others grow. Perhaps that's part of my soul's journey through this tragedy and grief. To share. I'm coming to see that it is an opportunity to help others. As time passes and healing happens, I hope to rise to the surface and breathe.

21

GRIEF BOMBS

Even as I rocked on my knees, howling, I detected soft breathing behind the roaring. I leaned in, listened. It was the murmuring of ten million mothers, backward and forward in time and right now, who had also lost children. They were lifting me, holding me. They had woven a net of their broken hearts, and they were keeping me safe there. I realized that one day I would take my rightful place as a link in this web, and I would hold my sister-mothers when their children died. For now my only task was to grieve and be cradled in their love.

—Mirabai Starr, *Caravan of No Despair: A Memoir of Loss and Transformation*

Three weeks after Hugh died, Hughdad and I ordered a pizza and walked around that neighborhood until the pizza was ready for pickup. I was so numb that I couldn't feel my feet as they hit the ground. My senses were deadened; there was a big gaping hole in my heart. The only thing working was my brain, and barely. Thank goodness my breath knew how to breathe me. Hughdad and I both tried to make good conversation about something, anything—totally feigning interest in an ounce of what was going on in the world, in other people's lives. I felt like an actor, an impostor wearing a mask. Not alive, not dead. I don't know what I was.

How could I possibly work through this oppressive and paralyzing grief? You'll read it and hear it and know it a thousand times over that everyone deals with grief differently and on their own timetable. There's no right or wrong way to do it. I think the biggest truth is that you can't go around it; you just have to go through it. I read somewhere that you can't win against grief because you're the one doing it to you. I ponder the concept that you're the one doing grief to you. In the early days and weeks and months and years, it is such a physical, visceral assault on your being that it certainly doesn't feel like a choice. It so feels done to you. Down the road, I could make choices about what to do with my grief and how I let it affect me, and I can see my own role in it, but I couldn't at first.

Even now, years into my journey, after much healing has taken place, a grief bomb can come out of the blue and hit me unexpectedly. It can happen when I'm driving down beautiful Lake Washington Boulevard and see a group of twentysomethings having the time of their lives on a

gorgeous sunny summer day—grilling lunch, paddleboard-
ing, riding bikes, laughing and loving—something my boy
will never experience. It can happen when I see families
traveling together—something we will never again get to do.
It can be triggered by driving past the soccer fields where
Hugh used to play. Or seeing darling young children sing
in a Christmas program and remembering how sweet and
fun that stage was. Or seeing Hugh's shoes in his closet. Or
hearing a song he loved. Anything or nothing can trigger it.
It's happening right now as I write this.

In my spiritual hybrid, there are just some days for a
biblical God. Down-on-my-knees, praying-for-comfort-and-
help kind of days. Years ago, when meeting with one of our
kids' psychiatrist and discussing the challenges we were fac-
ing with all sorts of things, I asked the doctor, "What do
we do when our child is in such a bad place and we've done
everything we can, and we're scared about what might happen?" He calmly gave me the most nonmedical advice ever:
"Embrace the Serenity Prayer," he said.

> *God, grant me the serenity to accept the*
> *things I cannot change, the courage to*
> *change the things I can, and the wisdom*
> *to know the difference.*

I harken back to that frequently when I'm experiencing
grief and don't know what to do. Maybe that prayer really
says it all.

My friend Sue sent me another article from the website What's Your Grief that has helped me in abundance and reframed my perspective on grief. The article is titled "Stop Trying to Heal from Grief." The author, Litsa Williams, MA, LCSW-C, says that if we think we must heal or recover from grief, it sets grief up to be an adversary, seeing it as a problem or threat to avoid. But if we change our language and thinking to something along the lines of "grieving is an ongoing and evolving process of healing," we might see that we heal *through* grief, that grief *is* the healing. The author writes, "And when I am no longer fighting against my grief, I am able to invite it in. I can listen to what it is teaching me about myself, about those I've lost, about how to live in this new world." Grief will most certainly be my lifelong companion, and it behooves me to see it in its ultimate healing light.

Through so much love and support, therapy, learning, my profound and transformative spiritual journey, it is now time for me to take my place as a link in the net of broken hearts, and to hold my sister-mothers and brother-fathers when their children have died.

I know with certainty that Hugh is taking his place in this lineage as well, he and I together. In addition to mediums telling me that Hugh is working with kids on the Other Side, I had beautiful confirmation of that in a reading my friend Ingrid and her husband, Monnix, had six weeks after their beautiful twenty-year-old daughter, Zoe, passed, two and a half years after Hugh did. It was their first reading with a medium, and they were understandably nervous, un-sure of what to expect, afraid that Zoe wouldn't be there. The medium, Joe, was highly recommended by Laura Lynne Jackson at her retreat I attended in New York, since she herself is no longer doing readings. A ringing endorsement from Laura Lynne is gold, and I passed along Joe's informa-tion to Ingrid.

In the reading, Joe pretty quickly determined that my friends had a child on the Other Side, but as he kept talking, he seemed to get the gender wrong. "You have a son on the other side."

"No," they responded.

Joe said, "OK, you have a daughter there. So please hold a second, because she's bringing forward a younger guy who passed. I don't know if this was a friend of your daughter's or whether you had a nephew who passed. But I've got a younger guy here."

Zoe and Hugh actually knew each other well in this life. Zoe's older brother, Finn, was a close friend of Hugh's in high school. Zoe had the incredible superpower of being able to calm Hugh during basketball games. He was an emo-tional player who could get so fired up at the refs, at other players, at unfairness, at himself, and Zoe would sit behind the bench and talk him off the cliff whenever he wasn't on the court.

Ingrid told Joe yes, that actually did make sense because there was a younger guy who passed who was a friend of Zoe's. Joe assured Ingrid and Monnix that their daughter would come through, but he wanted to see what this guy had to say, because he was the first one connected to them who was coming through. Joe provided information that this guy wanted his family to know he's watching over someone in his family whose name starts with *J-O* (Jordan!), and that his passing wasn't his fault or an intended thing. It was important to him that his family know that. By the symbolism Joe was getting, he had the sense that substances were involved, and he provided specific details of what happened medically at the young man's passing—specifics that Joe hasn't had come through before in a reading, and he didn't know why it was so important, but all of it was accurate. It left no doubt in my friends' minds that it was Hugh coming through. But why, when they were aching to hear from their daughter?

Zoe did come through, of course. She would never not. It was her first time. Slightly timid at first. Soft, then growing stronger and more confident as the reading went on—much as she was in life. Clearer and clearer information coming through. It was a beautiful reading that gave her parents tremendous comfort that she is very much here and still a part of their lives. My friends told me they are certain Hugh was there to support Zoe as she had supported him, and to show her how to do it, how to connect. And perhaps to show them, too, what to expect at a reading.

Hugh and I together, growing through the grief and heartache, taking our places in the web of support and love for others just like us.

22

HELPING
PARENTS HEAL

My early foray into grief groups was with an organization whose members had all lost someone to drugs or alcohol. I initially found comfort in knowing that everyone in the group understood and grappled with the same kind of grief that comes from losing someone to addiction. Each kind of loss comes with its special baggage. In one of the sessions, I shared about my experience in going to a medium. I felt timid mentioning it because things like that hadn't been discussed since I'd joined. Afterward, a couple of people contacted me with interest and wanted more information about going to a medium, but the group didn't generally go to that place. Over time, I wasn't interested in being in a group that was unified over the way our loved ones passed. I was well on my way down the spiritual path.

Back a ways in the book, I mentioned that during the Shift

Network's Beyond the Veil Summit, I was introduced to the name of Helping Parents Heal by Suzanne Giesemann. After googling the organization, I thought, *Holy cow, this is it.* Even the language used is different from other grief groups. They don't use words like "bereaved" or "lost a child," as the organization focuses on the hope that comes with acknowledging our spiritual nature and that we have a continued relationship with our loved ones after their physical death.

The HPH website is filled with resources that I soaked up—listings of books, videos, films, including a documentary that was made about seventeen parents from HPH who have a child that passed, titled *Life to Afterlife: Mom, Can You Hear Me*. In an interview-style documentary, the filmmaker talks with these parents about experiencing the unfathomable, and how they have been able to move from despair to hope and healing by continuing a joyous relationship with their children. That film was my first stop in the resources and spoke to the exact journey I am on. And all this in a grief group? I hadn't heard of any other like this, before or since. I found them eighteen months after Hugh passed, and I knew immediately that this was my place.

There is also a list of providers on the website, therapists and healers of different types and mediums who are tested, certified, and completely trustworthy. The mediums are tested by Mark Ireland, one of the cofounders of HPH. He is the son of well-known twentieth-century medium Richard Ireland and has been involved with research on mediumship at reputable universities.

HPH is an international nonprofit organization that was founded in 2012 by Elizabeth Boisson and Mark, both of whom experienced the passing of a child—and in Elizabeth's case, *two* children. The organization is dedicated to assisting parents by providing support and resources to aid in the healing process. It goes a step beyond other groups by allowing the open discussion of spiritual experiences and afterlife evidence, in a nondogmatic way. Affiliate groups welcome everyone regardless of religious (or nonreligious) background and allow for open dialogue.

I saw the website tab called "Affiliate Groups" and, upon checking it out, saw there was a group in Seattle. I emailed the leader and was disappointed to find that the group was currently inactive. Engagement had been low, and when the pandemic hit and the world went online, it just stopped. So, I continued with my journey of discovery by taking many courses and doing much reading.

But it kept nagging at me that Seattle could really use a group. I saw that HPH was growing and growing throughout the US and the world, and I couldn't believe there wasn't activity in Seattle. So, when I started to become certain that I wanted not only the support of the group but also to find a way to give back to others, I contacted the leader again and asked if she might like help getting it going again. We met for coffee, talked, and got excited about what we could do together. We became coleaders of the Seattle Affiliate Group, now three years after Hugh passed.

Seattle is a city of technology, data, and innovation with

it being the headquarters of Boeing, Microsoft, Amazon, numerous biotech firms, and a hub of so many more technology companies—not to mention Starbucks, Costco, and Nordstrom. It has historically been one of the most "unchurched" cities in the US, so I wondered if the spiritual nature of HPH would hit. But at the same time, Seattle is a very open minded and creative city, surrounded by the most divine natural beauty imaginable, with mountain ranges west and east of the city, 200 islands in the area, and lakes, rivers, and waterways everywhere. It is a city surrounded by water and the greenest of greens. It's no wonder it's called the Emerald City. People here are connected to nature, which I find to be the most spiritual experience of all. The Seattle group is growing. I would never want this club no one wants to belong to to get larger, but I'm so glad people have found us.

In our HPH meetings, we often have programming and speakers, discuss books, or have a sound healer or art therapist do a healing activity with us. In one of my favorite meetings, we watched a TEDx Talk together by Lucy Hone, PhD, called "The Three Secrets of Resilient People." Dr. Hone is a leading international resilience expert.

She opens the talk by telling the audience to stand and stay standing "If you've:

- ever lost someone you truly love,
- ever had your heart broken,
- ever struggled through an acrimonious divorce, or

- been the victim of infidelity . . .
- lived through a natural disaster,
- been bullied or been made redundant . . .
- ever had a miscarriage,
- ever had an abortion, or
- struggled through infertility . . .
- had to cope with mental illness, dementia, some form of physical impairment, or cope with suicide."

At the end of the list, almost everyone in the auditorium is standing. She goes on to say, "Look around you. Adversity doesn't discriminate."

She tells us about how she thought the defining moment of her resilience expertise was when the big earthquake hit her native Christchurch, New Zealand, in 2011. She poured herself into working in her community with many organizations to help teach people the ways of thinking and acting that build resilience. She thought that was her calling, her moment to put all her research to good use.

But her true test came in 2014 when her twelve-year-old daughter, Abi, was killed in a car accident, along with Abi's best friend and her best friend's mother. Dr. Hone was thrust to the other end of the grieving spectrum, where now people were telling her that statistically her marriage would end in divorce, that her family was at high risk for mental illness, and that she would probably write off the next five years of her life to grief.

As we sometimes hear with experts, when people are personally put in the situation they usually help others with—something like tragedy—they don't know if they can apply their own expertise to help themselves, because they are human. Such was the case with Dr. Hone, but she applied her knowledge, and her talk was on the three strategies that got her through her darkest days:

1. Resilient people know that shit happens, and that suffering is part of life. She never did think "Why me?" Instead, "Why *not* me." Think of that room where everyone who had experienced deep hardship in their lives was standing. She was not immune to that.

2. Resilient people are really good at choosing where they put their attention. They recognize the things they can change, and accept those they can't. This is a learnable skill. And being able to switch your attention to the good and grateful has been scientifically shown to be a powerful strategy.

3. Resilient people ask, "Is what I'm doing right now helping or harming me?"—the way I'm acting, or thinking, or what I'm doing. This is a great question to ask ourselves in grief and in any aspect of our lives, and puts us back in the driver's seat of our life.

Dr. Hone has beautiful examples of how she put these strategies into action. She doesn't pretend that this takes away the pain, but the strategies are very helpful and have shown her that she can grieve and live at the same time.

I see resilience in abundance when I look at the faces of the parents in our Helping Parents Heal group. They have experienced the unthinkable. A couple of the families have had two children pass—similarly losing young kids to cancer and, later, college-age kids to suicide. One parent has three sons in spirit. *Three.* And yet, they move forward with grace and hope. A big part of that for us is in the knowing that our kids are right here, right now, walking alongside us. We see the signs of that everywhere.

You know the joyous feeling when someone you care about wholly gets you? You are seen and heard and felt, and they even know things about you that you don't notice yourself—and they unconditionally love you, warts and all. They are there to help you become your best self. That is what I have come to learn about my son and other loved ones on the Other Side, through profound evidence presented during mediumship readings—that Hugh, my grandparents, my dear in-laws, my aunts, uncles, cousins, friends who have crossed over see me, hear me, and know everything going on in my life. They know me better than I know myself, and they have so much love for me and are here to help guide me. That brings me tremendous peace and assurance that our relationships continue—those bonds are never broken.

It wasn't until much later in my journey and my development as a medium that I realized our loved ones in spirit have those same desires to be seen, heard, and felt by us. Imagine the elation they feel when we finally, *finally* recognize the communications they have been working so hard to show us. They want us to know they are very much still here, haven't gone anywhere, and love us dearly. They want so much for the relationship to continue and to grow. Some people see the signs of their loved ones immediately. I did not, until an outside influence—my colleague—got a message to me from Hugh that started the long journey of me opening up. My loved ones had to wait for me a long, long time.

Sometimes, at our HPH meetings, we simply use the time to check in, see how people are doing, and speak whatever is in our hearts. The conversation always, *always* turns to the signs we're getting from our kids. And let me tell you, our kids are creative and brilliant. You can see the transformation in parents as they talk about this. The smiles and laughter come out. I know our children are jumping for joy and high-fiving each other as the parents share and *talk* about this. We are acknowledging that we experience the communications from them. I originally started volunteering as an HPH affiliate-group leader because I have a deep passion for helping parents who are on this journey. I now know that we are serving the children in spirit every bit as much.

23

NEVER SHOULD I EVER NEED MORE PROOF THAN THIS

"You don't need to come, Hugh," I whispered. "I know you're here. It's more important that other kids come through and provide healing for their parents."

As coleaders of the Seattle Affiliate Group of Helping Parents Heal, my partner, Beth, and I started bringing in HPH-approved mediums a few times per year to do gallery readings at our monthly meetings. In a gallery reading, the parents are there on Zoom, and the medium brings through their children in profound ways. I have witnessed trans-formations, as many of the parents are hearing from their children for the first time. The medium can't control which children come through—they just present the information they are receiving until a parent raises their Zoom hand to say they can understand the information, and then the medium knows to connect more deeply with that parent as their child comes through, providing beautiful messages of hope and healing.

Of course, every parent wants their child to come through, but not all the kids do. There are many reasons for that—a couple being that we are the same people in spirit as we are on earth, and some kids are shy, or there may be circumstances around their death they don't want a group to know. If your child doesn't come, you have to trust that if it's true for other parents that their child is right here, yours is, too.

Hugh never comes through in group readings like this, and I'm OK with that because I've had so many experiences that show me he's here. And besides, tonight I am angry with him. As the layers of his life are peeled away after his passing, I am finding out things about him that upset me. Things he did. And the grace and emotional intelligence he extended to others didn't always translate to family. When he was younger, I even asked him, "Hugh, why are you so kind to other people and so mean to us sometimes?"

"Because I know you'll love me no matter what," he said.

Especially in his short addiction before passing, Hugh did some bad things. Anyone who has loved someone with an addiction knows the pain. The deceit. The manipulation. The stealing. It's not them. It's the disease that has taken over. And the past few weeks—now three years after Hugh passed—I was sad, disappointed, and mourning the person he was before all the Troubles. I hit a rough patch in my relationship with my son. I was hurting and honestly didn't want to hear from Hugh—not so unlike the tension a parent and child might feel about each other at any time.

It was fifteen minutes before the HPH meeting, and the medium, Jennifer, joined Beth and me a little early on Zoom. There was some chitchat, then down to the business of preparing for the parents to hop on the call shortly. Jennifer said, "As hosts, you probably try to defer to other people's kids coming through, but if you can take the information coming through tonight, you should claim it." Then she said she's never actually said that to the hosts of any meeting before, so there must be a reason. "Maybe spirit is already at work!" She laughed.

I could sense the anticipation and nervousness of the parents, even across the airwaves. Jennifer gave an introduction and set expectations, and said she was already sensing the kids. The first child in was claimed by his mother, Sarah. Her son, Xander, was in his late teens when he passed from an accidental overdose.

Jennifer brought through highly specific information about Xander. She saw a wig, which made Sarah laugh because Xander was a goofball and once wore a wig during a soccer game. Jennifer also saw a logo of some kind. Sarah commented that, wow, she just had a logo developed for the charitable work she's doing in Xander's name. Sarah said she and Xander are "working together" on community involvement. So, Jennifer established quickly that she's the real deal. And Sarah was overjoyed.

I felt a synchronicity with the messages that came in for Sarah. Jennifer asked, "Are you writing a book about your son, or about what you're going through?" Sarah said she had written one chapter about Xander for a book collective. "You are really going to make a difference, more than you'll ever know. You're going to have a big audience, masses of people. You're not interested in your current career anymore; you want to move in a new direction." Sarah couldn't take the last bit. I don't think she's working outside the home. I could certainly take that, and I was also writing a book about my son and what I'm going through. In gallery readings, it's said that the spirits can piggyback on each other, giving messages that are relevant to more than one person.

In the middle of that reading, Jennifer said, "Is anyone here connected to April? April 27, specifically?" Wow, yes, that was Hugh's fateful night. Incredible. I raised my Zoom hand. "OK, Wendy, I'll get back to you." Then a few minutes later, she asked Sarah, "Did Xander have a friend who also passed from an overdose? He's bringing someone else in. They're playing around, pushing each other to the front." Sarah said no. Jennifer asked the group, "Did anyone else have a son pass from an accidental overdose?" I raised my Zoom hand again. "OK, I'll come back to you."

When Jennifer finished the beautiful reading with Xander, she called me out. "When your son comes through, he looks down. That means to me that he's either shy (he's not) or choosing his words carefully. He wants you to be proud of him.

"He's saying, 'I know there are some things where I didn't make you so proud of me.'

"'I know there are some things I said and did, and that I didn't accomplish.'

"'My acts and my decisions were mine. They weren't because of anything you or anyone else said or did.'

"'There was no intention that I was to leave.'

"'I will take the rest of your physical lifetime to show you that you raised a good son.'

"And he's saying, 'Mom, I know there's one thing you've been waiting to hear—I'm so sorry.'"

The readings I've experienced, and certainly in these group readings, have typically been filled with light and love. This was different—it was earnest, contrite, urgent. And it 100 percent addressed what had been going on in my head about Hugh over the previous couple of weeks, which I hadn't mentioned to even my husband.

We record these meetings so parents can witness again the beautiful messages they received from their children. When I watched it over again, I saw in myself a woman with a clenched jaw. A woman fighting back tears. I'm sure other people saw that in me, too, and were curious what those messages were about.

To me, more than anything, they were ultimately about proof. Proof that Hugh knows my every thought, my every action, and could speak to that. How could I ever doubt again?

24

SIGNS

I had a beautiful and unexpected conversation about grief with our housecleaner, Devon, one day, about eighteen months after I started coleading Helping Parents Heal. She was new to us, this being just the third time she'd been in our home. We liked her from the first moment she walked through the door because she has great energy. I've used that phrase "someone has great energy" many times in my life, but it's not until this journey that I've thought so deeply about how we each, honest to goodness, *are* energy and put out a palpable energy that others perceive. Hers is really up-beat, fun, kind. She's got a great laugh. She is mother to two young boys, one with a disability, so I know her life is chal-lenging, but she fills the room with goodness. It was won-derful to have her in our house.

She'd met all three of us in this household, including Hugh's sibling, Jordan. The house is loaded with photographs of both of our kids, but she has met just one. She likely thought the other was living elsewhere, maybe away at college. Jordan is an excellent cook and baker, and whipped up some amazing seasoned smashed potatoes for all of us—including Devon—to share, so we were all in the kitchen. Devon sang Jordan's praises and thought it was so great that a young person was into cooking. We were all enjoying the little bit of community right there, so I said, "You may have noticed the plaque in the living room for our son Hugh, who passed away."

My family had a beautiful, really heavy marble plaque made for us that sits in an easel on a shelf. It shows a close-up of Hugh's beautiful face from one of our vacations, with a massive Alaskan glacier behind him, and it says:

1999–2020
HUGH T SAFFEL IV

———

IF LOVE COULD HAVE
SAVED YOU,
YOU WOULD HAVE
LIVED FOREVER.

"Yes," Devon said. "I just really noticed that for the first time about ten minutes ago when I was in there dusting." I told her a bit about Hugh and that he had passed from fentanyl poisoning. She was very kind and empathetic. Then a tear rolled down her cheek, and she said, "My mom passed away just two months ago, on Halloween day, and I'm lost." Her mom had had breast cancer many years ago, followed by twelve years of remission, then it came back, spreading throughout her body. Devon and her mom were really close. Her mom was just fifty-nine when she passed.

I gave her a hug and decided to share a bit of my journey to healing and what has brought me comfort, in hopes that it might bring her comfort, too. I was beginning to see firsthand how helpful it was for grieving parents to learn more about mediumship and all that I was learning. Also, it was the perfect time to try my elevator pitch for this book, which I had been working on. "Elevator pitch" is the metaphor used to describe a scenario where you miraculously find yourself in the elevator with someone important and have the opportunity to sell yourself or your idea in a thirty-second elevator ride. Maybe you've bumped into the CEO of the company you work for, and you've been wanting to tell her about your big idea and would never otherwise have access to someone at that level. Or maybe you're writing a book about the aftermath of your child's death and how he found a way to get a message to you, which launched you on a massive spiritual journey that led you to know and experience the fact that our loved ones are still right here in every possible way except their bodies—and that they see you, hear you, guide you, and that the relationship continues. And you need to have a concise, compelling answer when someone asks, "What is your book about?"

Devon was really interested in my story, and it aligned with her beliefs about there being something beyond this life, something that continues, and the hope that her mom is still near. I told her that her mom wants to communicate, and I encouraged Devon to look for signs her mom is sending her, to show Devon that she is indeed here. "What signs do I look for?" Devon asked.

Oh, wow, yes, that's a good question, and something to explore here. I've mentioned the signs I've asked Hugh for, and have gloriously received. And the cherries that my colleague told me would be a sign from Hugh, and how those played out. But what do you look for, and what do the signs mean?

In an interview about her research on mediums, Dr. Julie Beischel talks about the signs we get from our loved ones and says, "You are probably looking for *fireworks*, when you should be looking for *fireflies*."

Seeing signs and trusting them is something I've been learning a lot about and have spent a lot of time discussing with the parents at HPH meetings. A good rule of thumb is to notice when something snags your attention—it's unusual, or unexpected, or a coincidence, or it reminds you of your loved one. If you think it might be a sign, it is.

These are some of the common signs that spirit is so good at sending:

1. **Disruptions with electricity and electronics:** spirit is energy and can manipulate energy, so you may get flickering lights at opportune times; or your TV—which has been in sleep mode—suddenly bursts on in full volume when

you ask your husband, "I wonder if Hugh will be at his memorial service"; or when your family is over for Christmas and you somehow get on the topic of hairless cats and you're looking in your phone's photo album for that awesome photo of your friend's hairless cat that looks like a gray web-footed alien with huge eyes and tufted ears, and you select that photo but instead up pops a photo of your son, which was nowhere near that cat photo in your album. Just sayin'.

2. **Animal signs:** There's a reason certain critters are often seen as signs from our loved ones—butterflies, dragonflies, ladybugs, birds, deer—because they are apparently easily manipulated by energy. I remember a warm summer night when Hugh's girlfriend was at our house sometime after his passing. She is so dear to us. We were eating dinner outside on the patio—a beautiful night under the stars and our party lights. She seemed a little nervous. She told us she wanted to date again, and I know she was concerned about hurting us. A dragonfly, which we rarely see in our yard, was relentlessly flying just around her, circling her. It was quite something. We all knew Hugh was there and telling her that it's OK. That he supports it. That he wants her to be happy.

   One of the mediums I went to told me that

Hugh would send me the sign of birds with blue feathers. There aren't actually that many blue birds, and they are very regional. Who knew that Steller's jays would become one of our most precious signs from Hugh. I was on a walk once when seven of them came flying from behind, split around me, and landed in the tree right in front of me—at a time when I needed them on my sad, reflective walk. And I so often truly feel pulled to the window, and there will be a jay just a couple of feet away from me, sitting on the roofline. For my birthday, my husband gave me a beautiful small painting of a jay, and I wept.

3. **Repetitive numbers:** You may have heard about numbers being spiritual, particularly repetitive numbers like 111, 222, 333, etc. That has really been one of the signs I receive. I can't tell you how often I happen to look at the clock when it's 11:11 or 1:11, or when I make a purchase that ends up being $11.11 with tax. Or I get invited by a friend to go to dinner, and when I google the restaurant, the address is 1111 Fairview Ave N., or even when I'm in Cuba, riding in a cab on a rainy day, and I turn my head to the window just as we pass a house with the number 111. A medium I went to said that she saw numbers all around me. I told her I receive them all the time

and asked what the significance is. She asked my spirit people, and they said the numbers mean that "we" are there.

4. **Objects in our path that were important to them:** Feathers, coins, heart-shaped rocks, license plates with their name on it. I know several people who just keep finding dimes or feathers all over the place when they weren't just shortly before.

5. **Your loved one's favorite song, or their perfume, or cigarette smoke:** You hear or smell or see things that had great meaning to your loved one. I went on a walk with my friend Diana a few months after Hugh passed. We talked all the way about Hugh and about Diana's beloved father, who also passed—and about what we've been experiencing with them in spirit. It was quite a walk, as about midway, an adolescent boy on a bike stopped us and asked, "Do you know what happens when we die?" Diana and I looked at each other. Wow. Coincidence? Well, yes, we told him a lot about what we know happens after we die. That kind of stumped him, as it ended up that he'd approached us to evangelize his beliefs, so he got way more than he was expecting, for sure. But the real point of this story is that when Diana and I parted ways and she walked back to her house, truly out of

nowhere, she heard an accordion playing her dad's favorite song, one he himself loved playing on the accordion. It gave her such joy.

6. **Dreams:** Oh, how I wish I had more dreams of Hugh than I do. I've had exactly three, and they were brief. Each time, he's wearing his favorite white hoodie. Maybe he'll give me a hug, or kiss me on the cheek, and then he'll be gone. One of my friends has full-blown, lively conversations with her daughter in her dreams, which brings her so much happiness and peace. It is said that the hallmarks of visitation dreams are the following:

   - The dreams are extremely vivid and detailed—much more so than regular dreams—and they can stay with you for many months or years. They feel real.

   - Your loved one will appear to be healthy and loving—even if they weren't that way in life. They are now healed and whole, and they won't bring in any of the hard things you may have experienced together.

   - Their communication will be very clear, and reassuring—that they are fine and that they love you.

   - You won't have to wonder if it was a visitation dream. You'll just know it was.

   - When you wake up, you will feel at peace.

7. **Tingling, goose bumps:** I've heard some mediums call these truth shivers—when you feel the energy of your loved one and know they are there or that something you're thinking about or doing is right and you're being guided in some way. I'm feeling this more and more as I open up, and I love it because I'm not thinking about the connection. I'm experiencing it.

The signs really can be anything that has meaning to you and your loved one. Parents I know call their son James their skywriter, because he sends them the most amazing cloud formations. He loved medieval cosplay and jousting. The mom showed me a picture of him with his legs in a triangle stance, hand on hip, holding a sword out in front of him with his other hand. Then she showed me the picture of a cloud formation that looked exactly like that. It was incredible! And the other day, she got a perfect *J* of a cloud.

Another mom gets incredible signs from her son Lincoln, who passed when he was just fifteen months old. She experiences him as a much more mature soul than his tender young age. I'm always dazzled by the signs he sends her. Recently, she was met with a new opportunity at work, which she could accept or not. There were good things about it, but there were also some things that didn't feel quite right for her, and the momentum was moving toward her accepting it. She asked Lincoln for help. She told him, "If I'm not supposed to take this position, please give me the sign of a black Lincoln (car)." Then she thought, *No, I live near an air-port and see black town cars every so often.* So, she corrected her wish by asking her boy for the sign of a white Lincoln if she wasn't supposed to take the position and a blue Lincoln if she should accept. Later that day, she went to pick up her children from daycare and passed two black Lincolns and two white Lincolns. The next day, she gracefully turned down the opportunity. A few weeks later, a coworker offered her a different role, and no more than a few minutes later, an advertisement with a blue Lincoln showed up on her computer screen. She quickly accepted, and the position helped her build skills modeling her personal values in a corporate environment at a larger scale. It was exactly the right fit.

Our loved ones can even help us get great parking spots. That's what the daughter of another mom does. The mom says it happens without fail whenever she circles and circles with no luck in finding a place. She lifts that up to her daughter in spirit, and she gets *the* closest spot to the Costco entrance, even at 10 a.m. on a Saturday!

The most important thing is not to doubt what you're seeing, hearing, and experiencing. The more you notice those things, acknowledge them as signs, and thank your loved one for them, the more it opens the pathways of communication and the more you'll get. You can ask them for specific things, too—then be patient.

After talking about signs with Devon and being open about my journey, she thanked me several times. She said she doesn't have many people she can talk with about her grief, or who would understand. We agreed that our culture doesn't address grief particularly well, and that it's good to normalize these discussions since death and grief affect us all. She said, "I feel so much better. I can't thank you enough." May it be so for all of us, as we open up and dare to be vulnerable, to connect with others on this shared journey.

25

NEAR-DEATH
EXPERIENCES

I almost died when I was twenty-nine. I have no idea why I almost did or why, under the circumstances, I didn't. I've had asthma since childhood, and a lot of allergies, and was a pretty sickly kid. My asthma was exercise induced, but I really had the most trouble with it when I got a respiratory virus. A regular cold to some would become a worry-filled thing for me. Those childhood episodes were in the days before bronchodilator inhalers, so when you had an asthma attack, you'd ingest a pill, and it would take forty-five minutes to get relief. Meanwhile, breathing could get very scary. My asthma got better in adulthood, but I still have to take good care when getting a cold or bronchitis.

On this particular day, I woke up with a cold and felt the familiar raw, burning heaviness in my lungs. I called in sick to work, made an appointment with my doctor, and got the usual prednisone that would keep my lungs from becoming inflamed. I went home and did all the things I always do. Drank a ton of warm water, took a variety of over-the-counter remedies for symptomatic relief, and rested. I fell asleep for a much-needed nap and woke up really struggling to breathe. Now, there were great inhalers that brought relief, which really worked, but not this time. I felt like I was suffocating, and I was scared. What saved me was that I lived in an apartment building directly across the street from the emergency room of a major hospital on Seattle's First Hill—nicknamed Pill Hill because of all the hospitals and medical facilities in the small neighborhood just off of downtown. I stumbled over to the ER, and was immediately taken to a room. A nurse took my vitals, and when she left the room to get something, I felt my vision closing in with blackness—like at the end of a Looney Tunes cartoon when it says "That's all Folks!" and blackness moves from the edges of the screen to the center until there is only a pinhole of light left. Which eventually closes completely.

I woke up three days later in a hospital room, completely disoriented. The nurses told me the harrowing tale of how I almost didn't make it. I had gone into respiratory arrest, and when they intubated me, my lungs were rigid for a reason no one could explain, and when they tried to push oxygen in, it blew holes in my lungs, and both collapsed. I'd spent the last three days in the ICU. I had apparently woken up enough at some point to write out the phone numbers for my work and my mom, who was on her way up to Seattle. I now understand what a terrifying phone call that must have been for her to receive.

I remember absolutely nothing about those three days in the ICU. I was heavily sedated. The nurses gave me the many sheets of paper on which I had written some communications, since I was intubated and couldn't talk. I was clearly terrified. I thought I was dying. I wrote dark things, and had scribbled "AFGO" in several places, which was the acronym my mom, a counselor, used for those really difficult experiences in life. Another f*cking growth opportunity.

I was in the hospital for two weeks while the surgical team and internal medicine team duked it out over what the best course of action was to get my lungs to reinflate. On the daily rounds, one team would turn the suction up on the tubes in my chest to fully inflate the lungs. Then the other team would come in later and turn the suction down to get my lungs to deflate a little, with the belief that they would fold over themselves and heal the holes. I could hear them arguing in the hallway. After two weeks, my lungs still weren't fully inflated, and they decided to send me home with the tubes still hanging out the sides of my chest, with flutter valves at the end to let air that had leaked into my chest cavity from my holey lungs escape. I did heal from that terrifying episode, and astoundingly, after that whole ordeal, I've not had asthma since.

Although I don't remember anything about the crisis, I had the profound sense of being saved. I knew I had been, and that knowing stays with me still. For a long time afterward, I was filled with deep gratitude for just waking up every morning, knowing now that this isn't to be taken for granted. I remember slowly moving my hand over the spines of my books and the trinkets that reminded me of memorable experiences, savoring photographs, soaking in my life—certain there had been Divine intervention.

A beautiful life-changing thing that came from my health crisis was my now husband. Hugh and I worked together at an advertising agency, and he was a wonderful colleague, so well liked by everyone. Creative. Hardworking. Warm. Hilarious. Dependable. Good to the core. We had a budding friendship, as I'd only been at the agency for about six months. When I was hospitalized, he came out of the woodwork to help me. He came to the hospital almost daily, bringing me books, video games, carrot cake, and we just sat and talked. That was all very unexpected. The first weekend I got out of the hospital, he asked me out on a date, and we've been together ever since. He says his parents always told him not to go for fast women, so he went for one who was sick and slow.

I lived for years not knowing for what purpose I had been saved. After getting married, when Hugh and I were in the situation to adopt our children, I had the belief that the purpose was to be a mother to these two beautiful children who were coming into the world anyway and needed one—and I have worked so, so hard to be the best mother I can possibly be. After son Hugh died, it totally shattered my sense of purpose. Isn't the number one responsibility of a parent to keep their children safe and healthy? I couldn't, and didn't, save my son. What then could my purpose possibly be? I still struggle with that. Is it this, right here, right now?

Even though my near-death experience (NDE) was a big black hole, for millions of other people, their NDEs have been profound, sometimes well-documented, much-researched spiritual experiences that show us so much about the afterlife and give us a glimpse of what our loved ones on the Other Side experienced in their transition. Learning about these experiences is something that often brings great comfort to many people in grief. It is a topic that sometimes comes up at our Helping Parents Heal meetings.

The term "near-death experience" was coined in 1975 by Dr. Raymond Moody in his book *Life After Life*. He was just a young medical student when he first started hearing stories from patients who had died and were resuscitated. There were unique aspects to each person's story, but many similarities also: He consistently heard "descriptions of a beautiful realm where patients were welcomed by deceased loved ones and 'beings of light.' Patients described leaving their bodies, being able to see from a vantage point above and then traveling down a tunnel or a canyon, joined by loving guides." As I've heard many mediums describe, Dr. Moody said that people talk about a life-review process, where they reexperienced events from their life and felt both the pain and joy they brought others. "Some patients' NDEs had all of these touch points, others only a few, but the majority described their NDE as being ineffable, filled

with love, comfort and awe that could never be fully captured in words." He has heard thousands of these stories.

Medical science often explains these as being hallucinations of a dying mind. But then along comes Dr. Eben
Alexander, a neurosurgeon who had an NDE of his own.
He was an academic neurosurgeon for more than twenty-
five years at very notable hospitals, as well as at Harvard
Medical School. In interviews I've seen of him, he says he
spent fifty-four years of his life honing a very scientific
worldview, teaching neuroscience, thinking that the brain
created consciousness. He fully bought into the conven-
tional scientific notions of materialism or physicalism that
only the physical world exists, that the brain creates consciousness. His NDE showed him very profoundly that this
is completely false. That our soul is a very real concept.
Evidence is everywhere that the brain is not the creator of
consciousness.

In 2008, he contracted a rapidly progressive case of
E. coli meningoencephalitis and descended quickly into a
weeklong coma. All his neurological exams, CT scans, and
cerebrospinal blood tests showed extensive brain damage,
and with his unresponsiveness to IV antibiotics, that put
his chances of survival at just 2 percent. In the days before
his meningitis started to subside, he had a remarkable experience of being in a valley filled with beauty and lights
and colors beyond what we can normally possibly see. Of
being accompanied by a young woman who never spoke,
but whose thoughts of unconditional love and assurance

came into his awareness and assured him of infinite healing. Of being schooled on the connectedness of all sentient beings and consciousnesses, and to the Divine. He describes in detail his experience in his book *Proof of Heaven: A Neurosurgeon's Journey into the Afterlife.*

After starting to come back to life, he said, "Initially, I was completely amnesic for my life before coma. I remembered no words, no personal memories of my life, no religious or scientific concepts, and nothing about being human or existing in this universe. I did not recognize dear family members standing around my bedside. All I remembered was where I had just been, in an extraordinary odyssey that seemed to last for months or years—although it had all occurred within the seven days I lay unconscious in the hospital."

He had extraordinary memories of his time in the coma, and the experience proved impossible to explain as a simple brain-based phenomenon, which the medical field would describe as hallucinations, dream states, drug effects, or fabricating gaps in memory. Medicine says that the neocortex of our brain is necessary for the construction of consciousness, but the extreme severity of Dr. Alexander's disease ruled out his neocortex as being able to generate memories at that time. He said, "Thanks to its preferential destruction of the neocortex, severe meningoencephalitis is, essentially, a perfect model for human death. That fact would nominate the disease for widespread study in brain-and-consciousness research, save for one problem: It almost always results in death. Almost no one returns to tell the tale."

His further deep science–based inquiry into his experience, and laying out all the reasons why science can't explain what happened, continued to comfort my fact-based, research-oriented self. I appreciate that there is logical thinking and research behind this, even if there aren't clear answers.

And then as a grieving mother who has lost a child, a great comfort for me came from one of the most incredible descriptions of an NDE I've heard, from a woman named Rosemary Thornton, who was clinically dead for ten minutes after bleeding out following a minor procedure related to her cancer diagnosis.

In online interviews, she describes being catapulted out of her body, like toast out of a toaster. She knew what was happening. There was no confusion. She had conversations with herself while this was all happening and even made jokes with herself. She was aware that every single thing she is was making the transition, and that gave her so much comfort: her macabre sense of humor, her goofiness, her thinking, her memories. She could hear herself giggle at herself even though she didn't have a body to make the laugh, but she was still producing and hearing sound. And she remembered thinking, *What did I leave on the gurney? The guilt. The self-recrimination, the anxiety, the sadness, the pain, the regret, every negative emotion you can imagine is what I had left behind.* She shed all that. She remembers thinking that she liked the feeling that she's not that person. She's not her fears, her worries, her woes. And she felt like none of the drama of her life was a big deal at all.

As she floated further and further away from what had been, she felt the presence of spiritual beings, and they were so glad to see her. It was like welcoming someone who's been away on a long voyage, and the three words that summed it up for her were "Welcome home, dearie." She had always felt like an oddball in life, but here she was with these beings that were so proud of her. So happy to see her back. The predominant feeling was of peace being infused into every iota of who she was. She couldn't describe what it was like because it surpasses what we can understand.

She was so happy she didn't have to start chemo the following week. And that there were no financial obligations anymore. She was so happy to be *done*. After a beautiful journey with these loving beings and something akin to a spiritual car wash, she was met with a white door, and she knew the door was the thing that would get her out of her earthly life. If she crossed through that door, she would be completely free. She was told that whatever decision she made, she would be so deeply loved—and if she decided to go back, she would be restored to wholeness. She was so filled with love and light and joy and freedom, and wanted nothing more than to go through the door.

As she put her hand on the door, she had a vision of the motherly nurse who had held her hand while she was bleeding to death. Rosemary had asked her, "Am I going to die?" The nurse said, "Oh honey, we're not going to let you die. We have many solutions for this." Rosemary was able to see with clarity the nurse now crying uncontrollably in a hospital supply room, head in hands, saying, "I promised that woman that I wasn't going to let her die, and I've lost her." Rosemary literally felt the grief and regret and sadness the nurse had in her. Rosemary had experienced a lot of emotional pain in her life, and she thought that if she could spare one human being that much pain, she had to go back. She took her hand off the white door, and she was back in her body in a millisecond.

After Rosemary's recovery, she had many tests done that showed there were no longer any signs of cancer or of heart damage from her ordeal, when her heart and brain had been without blood and oxygen for ten minutes. I've watched and read about many NDE stories through TEDx Talks, news programs, and books, and this is one of the most remarkable.

Back to Dr. Eben Alexander for a moment: When word got out in his hometown about his near-death experience, families he knew who had lost a child gained a lot of comfort from the talks he was giving. That fueled his interest in sharing his story with the world—the fact that bereaved parents were benefiting from this knowledge.

I have wondered why hearing about NDEs brings so much comfort to those who have lost someone. What I gain from Dr. Alexander's story, Rosemary's story, and so many others' is that no one dies alone. Ever. Each of our loved ones were met by family, friends, and loving beings overjoyed to see them. Our loved ones experience more love, more peace, more comfort, more beauty, more light on the Other Side than can ever be expressed by our language. And they are freed from all pain and worry. The same will be true for us, and that helps me not be fearful of death, for my son or for myself. Rosemary's story, in particular, also helps me understand what I have experienced in mediumship, that absolutely everything about a person, other than their bodies, is still accessible—consciousness, personality, memories, humor, interests. Everything about us makes that transition, and we are wholly ourselves. That is how and why people come through in a reading with such clarity, and why our relationships continue.

The hard part of all this for me is that many say we are met with a door where we can decide if we stay or if we go. Our soul may have decided about the departure point early on, but there is said to be free will at the time of departure. One medium told me that Hugh saw a door and took it. Other mediums have told me that Hugh's soul was stuck and that he needed to move on. Or that he had experienced everything here that he needed to, and wanted to be free. I am happy for Hugh upon getting these glimpses of the Other Side and of a soul's journey. I know he lives in indescribable joy, beauty, and peace. But I'm not happy for myself. Very selfishly, I wish he had chosen to stay here. I so miss that boy. Interestingly, I have had readings as well where Hugh specifically said that he wanted me to know he didn't choose to leave me. Maybe someday I will understand.

But the real beauty of near-death-experience stories is that they help me understand what happened for Hugh when he crossed over. They help me feel less afraid of my own death and less fearful that Hugh's experience was painful or frightening. This brings me so much comfort, as it does for many who grieve. What a gift to get a glimpse of the transition and the Other Side through other people's experiences.

26

THE UNEXPECTED JOY OF 1,100 GRIEVING PARENTS IN ONE ROOM

Community is everything on a grief journey, or in any difficult thing you're going through. Everything. I have been richly blessed to have family and friends who have been there for me from day one when Hugh passed, who have supported my journey and are open to talking about anything I want to talk about, being open minded about the spiritual development I'm experiencing. I've spoken with parents who have lost friends after their child passed, friends who just faded away. I don't understand all the reasons for that. Maybe those friends are just so unsure or uncomfortable about what to say or do. Or are really afraid to talk about death. Or perhaps they think that losing a child is contagious.

In addition to my family and friends, I have found my people at Helping Parents Heal, and it was never so evident as at the biennial conference in Phoenix that I just returned from. I had been waiting for this for two years, ever since I joined Helping Parents Heal. Right before I joined, the conference had already sold out for that summer. I heard so many amazing things about it from other parents and was disappointed not to get to experience it myself. When I did attend this one, two years later, I understood, first of all, why they could only do it every two years, given the enormity of it.

One thousand and one hundred parents from all around the world. Some of the biggest speakers in their fields of science, near-death experiences, healing modalities, mediumship. Programming ran from 8 a.m. to 9 p.m. every day. There was also a full day beforehand of breakout sessions and special panels. And there were just two people responsible for planning the entire event—Irene Vouvalides, the HPH Conference Chair, and Elizabeth Boisson, the HPH President. I volunteered to help during the conference. I assisted parents as they checked in. I saw what they looked like walking in, and I saw what they looked like walking out on the last day, and I can tell you that lives and grief were transformed.

How? Why? So many reasons. On the most basic level, a parent I talked with pointed out that our only job and identity there was as the parent of our child(ren) who had passed. We weren't navigating any of the other parts of our lives as employees, bosses, friends, neighbors, caregivers, community activists. I was there as Hugh's mom, with a beautiful picture of him on the three-inch button we each received with our child's picture—worn on top of my heart for four days. There was also never an elephant in the room. I heard parents talk about how in other parts of their lives, their child's passing felt like a weight that other people didn't quite know what to do with. Here, we all completely got each other. We could talk about our child and grieve and cry and laugh freely. And as I sat in the sound-healing lounge, watching the slide show of all the children represented there, I was overcome by the beauty of every one of them, each so loved and missed, and still so present. We were there, attending, with our children.

The brilliant programming of the conference proved that to me over and over again. As I just finished writing the chapter on near-death experiences, I want to continue on that thread for a moment. Three extremely well-known near-death experiencers did keynote presentations. They are people who have done TED Talks, have been highly sought-after speakers, have authored books about their experiences: Anita Moorjani, Jeff Olsen, Dr. Mary Neal. Each of them suffered excruciating, traumatic injuries or illness that led to their death, before eventual resuscitation. Each of them had profound experiences of love, peace, reflection on their lives, and spiritual accompaniment as they crossed over— just as Dr. Eben Alexander and Rosemary Thornton had. Each was told that it wasn't their time and that they had to go back to their bodies. None of them wanted to. They were incredible glimpses of what happens when we die, and were stories of finding strength and perseverance and ultimately of choosing joy when they survived.

Dr. Mary Neal said something that was really helpful to me. She is an analytical, spiritually skeptical orthopedic spine surgeon who died while kayaking in a Chilean river. She was an experienced recreational kayaker on vacation with her husband and friends, and they knew the challenges of this river. But even though prepared, something happened that flipped Mary's kayak over and got her pinned, and she drowned, spending thirty minutes underwater without oxygen. She described how she could feel her bones breaking and thought she should be screaming but felt no pain, no fear, no panic. She never felt dead. Only alive, then more alive than she had ever felt. The thing that touched me is when she said that no matter what we imagine our child's death and last moments to be, it's probably not at all the way they experienced it. I have imagined this often for Hugh, even though he actually told me in a mediumship reading that there are better things to think about and that I should stop doing that— as he also referenced a very specific detail of how I found him, so I know it was coming from him. So, I repeat this to myself—no matter what I imagine Hugh's last minutes to be, he probably didn't experience it that way at all.

The brilliant Dr. Gary E. Schwartz presented on "The New Science of the Soul," and there were other science-based presentations that had me enrapt. There were sessions on meditations and tools to connect with our children. And there were the mediums: Suzanne Giesemann, Gordon Smith, James Van Praagh, Maureen Hancock, and the gifted, tested, and certified Helping Parents Heal mediums, who gave many readings in large and small group settings.

I didn't hear from Hugh, but you've just got to know that a reading for one is a reading for all, when there is so much proof that other people's kids are here, so yours is, too. I was so happy for those parents and was moved to tears at times when I saw them physically change after hearing from their child, walking out of the room with joy in their hearts. A parent I know who has struggled on the journey received a completely unexpected reading and said later, "I can now actually say that I am happy and that I love my life. I can move forward." Going to a medium is not the be-all and end-all in this journey, but it can be a profoundly transformational healer.

Suzanne Giesemann presented, using amazing examples from her readings and life, about all the ways our loved ones set us up to meet the people we need to meet, to have the experiences we're supposed to have, to end up at the places we're supposed to go. We are actually "unwitting stooges" in their plans to help us. Just look at all the synchronicities in our lives. I saw so many synchronicities happening at the conference when people just happened to sit down at a table where everyone had something really significant in common. Or were in a breakout group with people who ended up being from their own geographical area and were able to make wonderful new connections. Suzanne gave us another of her wonderful military-inspired acronyms: NOE. There is just "no other explanation" than that our loved ones are here and involved in our lives. And she reminded us that our kids know *everything*. They know we had popcorn last night. They know we just wrote lyrics to a song this morning. They know about the new grandchild.

I was so waiting for a sign from Hugh while there. Surely, he must comply. He couldn't *not*, given the nature of the conference and since I was feeling very sad at times— which of course he knew. I went to a session on connecting with our children. We did a wonderful meditation where we envisioned meeting our child at a place of our choosing, and spending time with our child. I did clearly see in my mind a large white farmhouse set on acres of green, a cloudless sky, sun shining, a cool breeze. As I sat on the front stoop, waiting, I saw Hugh approach, wearing the white hoodie he always wears when I see him in my mind. He carried a small white box. He didn't say a word. He just reached out for my hand, pulled me up off the stoop, and handed me the box. I opened it, and there was a tiny jar of honey in it, about two inches tall. I looked at it and closed the box, and we walked off hand in hand toward the fields. Then the meditation ended. It felt good. It felt real. I didn't know why he gave me a jar of honey.

As I left the meeting room and walked out through the main concourse, I veered toward a table where a parent had made a bunch of small, beautiful mixed-media cards that were there for the taking. They were each different from the next and had clearly been the maker's labor of love in honor of her child. I mindlessly grabbed one. They were all so lovely. As I continued walking, I looked down at the card, which had different types of colored, patterned, and textured paper, some ribbon, torn-out text from books and recipes—and stamps of bees over all of it. Seven bees to be exact. And a little paper cut-out headline that said "Be the Exception." I stopped and looked at it. It wasn't lost on me that I had just been wondering why Hugh gave me a jar of honey in my vision, and moments later, I was holding a card covered with bees. Was that a coincidence? Did all those cards have bees on them? Was that a theme? I turned around and went back to the table and picked up card after card—none of which had bees on them. I'd picked up the one. Damn. There I went again, having to prove to myself that this really was a sign for me. I continue to be me. Have I learned nothing at this conference and beyond about our loved ones setting up these amazing signs, and to trust them?

There were so many new friends made, so much learning and loving, and healing and laughter. One of my favorite quotes from the conference that I brought back with me came again from Dr. Mary Neal, evoking Albert Einstein's great scientific statement, "There is no dark. Only the absence of light." Of course, I had to look the quote up, and Einstein elaborated that one can't even study darkness, only light. That darkness is a term used by man to describe what happens when there is no light present. Dr. Neal used the quote in describing her life review at death, when she saw that all negative experiences and emotions she'd had about her life were shown to be only the absence of understanding and love about the situation, once she saw it from a different perspective.

I know there is a lot of darkness in our grief. What if we look at it from the perspective of how we have grown through it and because of it? How we have seen the hands of support extended to us? How we have chosen to help others? How we feel grateful for the day we have, because we know intimately that not a single one is to be taken for granted? And above all, what if we just let ourselves feel the beautiful, profound love we have for our child, or spouse, or parent, or friend that has led to this moment of missing them. Therein lies the light.

27

TELL THEM THIS

Hugh's physical presence had been gone two years when I started writing this book. It has now been four. The passage of time and the hard-fought healing have allowed me to write from my scars instead of my wounds. Wisdom has had the opportunity to develop. After all is said and done—through my deep grief and quest to find a connection to my son; after the dive into the science and research of the afterlife and survival of consciousness; after all the summits, retreats, classes, and books; after studying and practicing mediumship—this is ultimately a story about love.

Not all the wisdom has been mine alone. In mediumship readings early on after Hugh passed, I received apologies for the pain and suffering Hugh had caused, acknowledgment that he was responsible for his passing, and powerful evidence that he's still here. That was what I needed at the time. In recent readings, I encounter a wiser Hugh, who continues to grow and learn on the Other Side. He comes through with support and encouragement for the things I'm doing and insight into my life, while still being his same self. Every medium I've gone to says that Hugh is an excellent communicator, that he's smart and funny, well liked, and still thinks himself quite handsome. They say he is really easy to read and makes their job easier.

In a reading with the gifted medium Joe, recommended by Laura Lynne Jackson, on the fourth anniversary of Hugh's passing—after Joe had brought through wildly accurate and specific information about Hugh, about things going on in my life, about trips I have coming up and just returned from, about the fact that I'm writing about Hugh—I asked Hugh what he thinks people really need to know in this book. Through Joe, my boy's words came tumbling out: "More than ever, people need to know and see what real love and a real family connection is—just by telling our story, just by sharing the truth. It might seem so mundane to you, like who would care, what are people going to learn from it? You don't realize how much love is in our family and how many people don't even know what that looks like. They can't recognize it or know they can have that. That's a big part of the lesson, of the wisdom. It's less about saying something that hasn't been said before, or a new revelation; it's more just about sharing our story and opening people's hearts and touching people."

Joe then asked me what the book is about. I told him it is the story of my journey with grief and the path to healing through the afterlife connection with my son. He said, "I think that goes along with what your son said. Even with the story you're telling, I think that at the end of the day, the heart has to be open. I always say about mediumship that love is the connector. I think that's what your son is saying, to show them the love. That's how this is all possible—it's through that connection. Show them the love that continues. You're proof that it works."

Yes, I see it now. This is absolutely a story about love and nothing else. My yearslong journey down an arduous and rocky road I never wanted to go on, to a place I didn't know existed, with my heart in pieces, has been solely about staying close to my son no matter what.

The journey has shown me that the Heaven I always thought was up there somewhere—where I would be reunited with Hugh again someday when I die—is actually not there, but here. Right now. I can have an active, two-way, mutually beneficial relationship with my son now, which continues to grow. I can communicate with him in a variety of ways, through a medium or not. I can get wisdom from him. I know he's actively involved and has full sight on my life, and is helping to guide me. And I cherish him more every day.

That is love.

28

MY EVOLUTION

Several mornings per week, I Sit in the Power, the practice to attune to the spirit world, to surrender and to ask for help in developing myself as I need to be developed. Afterward, I feel very connected to my spiritual center, and grateful, and humbled. Sometimes, I talk to my boy. Today, I reflected on the fact that I don't *feel* Hugh often. I can think of only three times when I had a sensation that I knew was him. I get many beautiful signs from him, but rarely sensations. I asked him if he could hug me.

I felt a thickening in the air around me and a pressure in my chest. Then a tightening in my body. I knew it was him. I sat. I soaked it up. I quietly cried. This was all miraculous and joyous enough, but then I started to see images in my mind.

I saw a series of black-and-white pictures that reminded me of the illustrated progression of human evolution, starting with the ape on the left through to the modern human on the right.

But in my vision, the first picture on the left was of a woman in a gray slip dress, desperately pulling herself up out of a swamp—gasping for air, nearly drowned, bedraggled, her long dark hair stuck to her face, her thin, weak arms and hands clinging to the reeds as if her life depended on it. Because it did.

The second picture was of the woman now fully on land, lying prostrate, arms outstretched, exhausted, breathing hard, covered with mud.

In the third picture, she had pulled herself up on her elbows.

Then to all fours, hunched over, breathing hard, her face still covered by matted hair.

Then in a crouch, her bare feet finally on the ground.

Her wobbling to stand up.

Taking her first step.

Stumbling, but moving.

Walking and weak.

Walking, her hand pushing the wet hair out of her eyes.

Walking.

Walking and strong. Back straight. Head high.

Walking with a smile, the sun shining on her face. Hope in her heart.

I knew that was me. My journey with grief. Four years later, I am strong and sure. I trip over sidewalk cracks sometimes. And the sun doesn't always shine. Sometimes, I'm struggling through the downpour and rolling thunder. But I am here.

I have the sense that at some point, I will run. And then I will fly.

My boy showed this to me.

Acknowledgments

"His death was my undoing and making."

—Medium Melissa Henyan,
on the death of her son

I must borrow this quote from Melissa Henyan, who is the talented medium I went to on my birthday two years after Hugh passed, and who delivered the pivotal message from him that I needed to write a book to help others. She was brought to her work as a medium after the passing of her son, just as I was brought to the writing of this book after the passing of mine. I didn't find this work—it found me.

To that point, the greatest of acknowledgments must go to my boy Hugh and my Grammy. Never would I have considered writing a book if not for their messages from the Other Side that I was to do so. In fact, if ever I would have considered it, I would have immediately discounted my ability or the possibility that I could have anything of value to say. This writing came from a great sense of obligation to them—and to all the beautiful souls on the Other Side who don't have a voice and who want more than anything for their loved ones to know they are still very much here, involved in our lives, and that they never actually left us.

As a first-time author, I was a deer in the headlights about what comes next after getting my blood, sweat, tears, and words on the pages. There's no way this would have become a book without my gifted editor, Gail Hudson—and it thrills me to no end to say "my editor." Who would have thought this would ever happen for me? She helped me take the disparate chapters I'd written and create a chapter map, ground it in a timeline, and show me where we needed connective tissue. She changed barely a word, but her impact was everything. I was introduced to Gail in the book-coaching program at Girl Friday Productions, who later ended up becoming *my publisher*—I love saying that, too. Having them publish my book wasn't a forgone conclusion. I am beyond grateful that they took me on and did what great publishers do: copyediting, proofreading, book cover and interior design, distribution, marketing. And they did it all with such care, thoughtfulness, professionalism, expertise, patience, and creativity. It was an incredible experience— one of the greatest gifts from this journey I'm on. Ingrid Emerick, cofounder and president of Girl Friday, friend, and fellow journeyer after the loss of a child, gave me endless encouragement, telling me that there is room for many stories whenever I questioned putting my book and myself out there in a market with many similar books.

I give a shout out to Seattle Public Libraries—and public libraries everywhere—for being safe, warm, quiet places for us to learn, read, write, research, study, and be in community with one another. I spent many hours at the library, getting out of my house for a change of scenery while writing, and marveled at the beautiful cross section of humanity all there together, sharing space that inspires and grows us as humans.

I give my wholehearted, love-filled thanks to my beautiful husband, Hugh, and kid Jordan—who are on a grief journey, too, although we each experience it differently—for their unending encouragement and support of my need to do this. Even though it meant seeing less of me over the last couple of years. Then again, maybe they're secretly happy I've had less time to wander the house, looking for things we can get rid of, because I hate clutter. "Do we need this?" They will probably put that on my tombstone.

And you, reader. You have so very many things and people needing your time and attention. And yet you made time to read this book. I am beyond grateful for that. And I'm so sorry for the events of your life that brought you to these pages. I am now so certain that as we share this same time on earth, we are part of the same fabric of life, and we matter to each other. I wish for you peace and the hopefulness that comes from experiencing that the relationship with your loved one continues.

Tips and Resources

LIKING THINGS IS GOOD ENOUGH, TO START WITH

A year and a half after Hugh passed, I was still feeling sad and hopeless quite a bit of the time. Kind of dead inside. Trying to manifest joy—my ultimate goal—right then felt unachievable. My therapist, Lindsey, suggested that instead of trying to do something or find something each day that brings me joy, how about doing something each day that I "like." That felt attainable. When focusing my lens on what things I liked in my days, there were many:

- I liked that I took a beautiful fall walk back from my therapy appointment, and went down some residential streets I've never been down before, and saw new things.
- I liked the delicious sausage, cheese, and broccoli egg bake that my husband made.
- I liked that I vacuumed and detailed the car.
- I liked that I felt competent in a new business task.

- I liked that I actually hit my target bedtime.

The list of things I liked every day was really long. I started paying attention to how I felt in those moments, and I actually got good feelings in my body that were peace or contentment or satisfaction, perhaps. Eventually, I noticed when I really actually enjoyed something, which grew to feelings of outright joy at times. But that didn't happen right away. Early on, liking things was good enough.

THREE THINGS I WANT PEOPLE WHO ARE GRIEVING TO KNOW

1. I know for certain that our loved ones on the Other Side want us to be healthy and happy, and to enjoy this life we have. At the beginning of the journey, I know you just can't imagine that's even possible. But for me, four years in now, I'm there. I've found tremendous healing in my journey and have received so much evidence that Hugh is right here, right now. I'm determined to live my very best life because I know he's watching and that he wants that for me. I want that for myself. And besides, our loved ones are more accessible to us when we aren't in pain. It's hard sometimes—I still cry every week, and I never know when a grief bomb will

hit, but I also feel so much gratitude and joy, and am moving forward with him alongside me.

2. Part of being able to move forward in life and to feel happiness is in developing a different relationship with grief than I initially had. As mentioned in an earlier chapter, grief is not an adversary. It's not the thing we have to heal from and get through. It *is* the healing and will be with me the rest of my life. I've learned that grief and joy can coexist. They are not mutually exclusive. They are both part of our emotional wheelhouse, and we have room for both.

3. The relationship with our loved one continues and even grows. Through mediumship, I know that Hugh is aware of everything about me— my thoughts, my actions, what's going on in my life. And he has given me good advice. In a way, we're even closer than when he was physically here. It's not the relationship with him I would have hoped for, but it's the one I have. It's sacred, and I will do everything I can to nurture that relationship.

"Grief is not a competition. Everyone feels their grief at 100 percent."

—Kathryn and Mitch Shirley,
grief recovery specialists, UK

I attended a great workshop on the importance of mediums understanding grief when giving readings, given by the wonderful Shirleys, who are not only grief-recovery specialists but also mediums. This quote from them was a good teacher for me. Losing a child is often said to be the greatest loss a person can experience in their life. That could be, but there are many tragedies in this world—and grief far broader than losing someone you love. People experience grief over the loss of health, or a job, or a relationship, or a home, or freedom. Grief over the loss of a beloved animal companion. Grief over climate change, politics, the future of our world. This quote helped me understand that it is all heartbreaking and all felt at 100 percent by the experiencer. It has helped me to hold compassionate space for anyone I speak with who is experiencing grief and not feeling like it can't compare to what I've experienced. Grief is a shared human experience, and we need to lift each other up, no matter the circumstance.

THE WEIGHT OF GRIEF DOESN'T GET LIGHTER, BUT YOU GET STRONGER TO CARRY IT

One of the wonderful parents in our local Helping Parents Heal group used the metaphor that grief feels like a brick in your pocket that at first you can't lift, and it feels paralyzing. As time goes by, your body and mind adapt and get stronger, and you find ways to carry the brick with you. And then perhaps at some point, you can't imagine life without that brick because the weight gives you comfort, as it's made with the love, bond, and memories you hold. That feels really true to my experience. That weight is always going to be there, but I've found ways to move forward, find purpose, and experience joy with that forever present.

RESOURCES

I have spent so many days, so many evenings, late nights going down rabbit holes online. One query leads to another, as I've worked to understand, educate myself, research the science, tie things together in my mind—so that I not only believe, but also know. I provide resources here I trust so you hopefully don't have to go down the rabbit holes, too.

Grief Support

Helping Parents Heal: helpingparentsheal.org
Helping Parents Heal (HPH) is a nonprofit organization dedicated to assisting parents whose children have passed. Through support and resources, HPH aspires to help individuals become "Shining Light Parents," meaning a shift from a state of emotional heaviness to hopefulness and greater peace of mind. HPH goes a step beyond other groups by allowing the open discussion of spiritual experiences and afterlife evidence in a nondogmatic way. HPH welcomes everyone regardless of religious or nonreligious background and encourages open dialogue.

Other Resources for Grief Support

- Forever Family Foundation:
  foreverfamilyfoundation.org
- What's Your Grief: whatsyourgrief.com
  - whatsyourgrief.com/he-was-a-million
    -other-things-overdose/
  - whatsyourgrief.com/stop-trying-to
    -heal-from-grief/
- Grief in Common: griefincommon.com
- Grief Recovery After Substance Passing
  (GRASP): grasphelp.org
- The Compassionate Friends:
  compassionatefriends.org
- Dr. Lucy Hone: drlucyhone.com
- Lifespan Integration: lifespanintegration.com
- EMDR trauma therapy—find a
  licensed therapist: emdria.org

In the event of a mental health emergency in the United States, if you or someone you know is considering suicide or self-harm:

- Call or text 988, the Suicide and Crisis Lifeline,
  or use the chat feature at 988lifeline.org.
- Text "HOME" to 741741.
- Go to the nearest emergency room.

Science

I provide here information about some reputable institutions and universities studying the survival of consciousness and the afterlife.

- Windbridge Research Center, with Dr. Julie Beischel: windbridge.org
- Laboratory for Advances in Consciousness and Health (LACH), Dr. Gary E. Schwartz, Director: lach.org
- University of Virginia Division of Perceptual Studies, studying extraordinary experiences: med.virginia.edu/perceptual-studies
- New York University's Parnia Lab, studying the experience of death and conscious awareness in an unbiased and methodical manner: med.nyu.edu/research/parnia-lab
- Yale University COPE (Influence/Control Over Perceptual Experiences) Project: powerslab.net
- Life After Life, the website of Dr. Raymond Moody and the pioneers who are following in his footsteps: lifeafterlife.com
- IONS (Institute of Noetic Science), founded by Apollo 14 astronaut Dr. Edgar Mitchell: noetic.org
- Academy for the Advancement of Postmaterialist Sciences (AAPS), inspiring

scientists in all areas to expand their theories, methods, and applications by exploring mind and consciousness as core properties of nature and the cosmos: aapsglobal.com

Dr. Gary E. Schwartz says there are huge amounts of evidence that, when put together, make an overwhelming evidential case for life after death. When you integrate all five areas of the research noted by the books below—none of which is definitive in itself—it's far beyond reasonable doubt. "In fact, the only way that you can doubt this, is to engage in *unreasonable* doubt."

- *Life After Life* by Raymond Moody, MD (on near-death experiences)
- *Hello from Heaven!* by Bill Guggenheim and Judy Guggenheim (on after-death communication)
- *Children Who Remember Previous Lives* by Ian Stevenson, MD, and colleagues at the University of Virginia (on reincarnation)
- *The Afterlife Experiments* by Gary E. Schwartz, PhD (research on and with mediums)
- The emergence of postmaterial communication technology as discussed in books by Dr. Schwartz: *Extraordinary Claims Require Extraordinary Evidence, Greater Reality Living,* and the upcoming *The SoulPhone Experiments*;

his article "Photonic Measurement of Apparent Presence of Spirit Using a Computer Automated System" was published in *Explore: The Journal of Science and Healing*

Spirituality

* The Shift Network: theshiftnetwork.com
* Younity: younity.com
* Laura Lynne Jackson: lauralynnejackson.com
* Suzanne Giesemann: suzannegiesemann.com
* Marie Manuchehri: energyintuitive.com
* Michael Mayo: mediummichaelmayo.com
* Oakbridge Institute: oakbridgeinstitute.org
* Arthur Findlay College: arthurfindlaycollege.org
* Find a Certified Medium by Mark Ireland: findacertifiedmedium.com/
* The NDE of Rosemary Thornton: youtu.be/aI-tACF9LFM?feature=shared
* The NDE of Jeff Olsen: youtu.be/1FD5lReqe64?feature=shared
* The NDE of Dr. Mary Neal: youtu.be/C-M9zR17egA?feature=shared
* We Don't Die: wedontdie.com

Credits

Chapter 8 (page 46): Laura Lynne Jackson quotes from *Signs: The Secret Language of the Universe* used by permission of Penguin Random House.

Chapter 9 (page 54): Laura Lynne Jackson quotes from *The Light Between Us: Stories from Heaven. Lessons for the Living* used by permission of Penguin Random House.

Chapter 12 (page 78): Julie Beischel, PhD, quote from *Investigating Mediums*.

Chapter 12 (page 85): Julia Assante, PhD, quote from *The Last Frontier* © Julia Assante, PhD. Used by permission of New World Library www.newworldlibrary.com.

Chapter 17 (page 139): "Protesters banned, arrested" cover article photography, Harry Soltes / *The Seattle Times*, 1999.

About the Author

WENDY JORDAN SAFFEL is an affiliate group coleader for Helping Parents Heal, an organization dedicated to assisting parents whose children have passed. She has worked in marketing for arts and tech for decades, and her writing has appeared in multiple publications. She lives with her family in Seattle. Find her online at wendysaffel.com.

www.ingramcontent.com/pod-product-compliance
Lightning Source LLC
Chambersburg PA
CBHW021233130626
46554CB00004B/1468